BUDDHA GAYA
THROUGH THE AGES

Bibliotheca Indo-Buddhica Series No. 134

BUDDHA GAYA THROUGH THE AGES

D.C. Ahir

Sri Satguru Publications
A Division of
Indian Books Centre
Delhi - India

Published by :
Sri Satguru Publications
Indological and Oriental Publishers
A Division of
Indian Books Centre
40/5, Shakti Nagar,
Delhi-110007
(INDIA)

First Edition : Delhi, 1994
B.E. 2538

ISBN 81-7030-409-1

Printed in India

PREFACE

This study presents a comprehensive and uptodate history of Buddha Gaya Through the Ages, from 528 BC to 1993 AD. The past history of the development; decline, discovery and restoration of the Great Maha Bodhi Temple is primarily based on the archaeological and inscriptional evidence found at Buddha Gaya itself, and which has been well-documented in the pioneer works of R.L. Mitra (1878), A. Cunningham (1892), and B.M. Barua (1934). For the century-old Buddhist revival movement initiated by Anagarika Dharmapala in 1891, I have relied heavily on the Maha Bodhi Journal, the spokesman in print of the Maha Bodhi Society of India since 1892.

As regards the present conditions at Buddha Gaya, I might add that during the last 24 years I have been to Buddha Gaya five times, and seen the changes taking place there. I first visited Buddha Gaya, along with my elder son, Nirmal, on 28 May 1971. On my return, I noted down in my diary as follows:

> "Reached Buddha Gaya on the morning of 28 May (Saturday). Stayed at the Maha Bodhi Rest House. Ven. Pannarama was very helpful. Worshipped at the Sacred Maha Bodhi Temple and collected some data from the office of the Management Committee about the present state of affairs. Not very happy with the desecration of the Temple being done by the Mahant. In particular, the Sivalingam in the main shrine is an affront to the Buddha and the Buddhists."

During my second visit to Buddha Gaya on 2-4 April 1979, I made a thorough survey of the Temple Complex, and other places associated with the Buddha. I again visited Buddha Gaya on 7-10 December 1982, 19-21 November 1989 and 7-10 December 1990. As such, much of what I write here is based on personal observation during these visits from 1971 onward. However, it has been further updated with the help of Ven. Dr. Rashtrapal Maha Thera, President of the International Meditation Centre, Buddha Gaya, and Shri M. Subba, Secretary, Daijokyo Buddhist Temple, Buddha Gaya. I am thankful to them.

The chapter on the recent turmoil at Buddha Gaya in the wake of the Buddhist agitation for complete control of the Maha Bodhi Temple (Mahavihara) is largely based on the objective reports published in The Times of India, New Delhi on the events during 1992 and 1993.

I am also thankful to Mr. K. Godage, Ambassador of Belgium whose article ''Restoration of Buddha Gaya'' published in the Special Number of ''Sambodhi'' in December 1991, has been included by me in Appendix I. Suggestions made by him need careful consideration by the authorities.

Lastly, I must thank my wife, Swarn Lata, who accompanied me to Buddha Gaya in 1979, 1982 and 1990, and helped me in various ways.

D.C. Ahir

Buddha Purnima,

1994

INTRODUCTION

Of all the places sanctified by their association with Gautama Buddha, Bodh Gaya or Buddha Gaya shines the brightest. Being the scene of Buddha's penance and enlightenment, it has always been the first choice of the pilgrims. Beginning with the visit of Asoka, the First Buddhist Emperor of India, in 260 BC, the streams of pilgrims flowed towards it without intermission for more than 1500 years. And "Princes from all parts of India vied with one another in enriching it with the highest treasures that they could command."

The magnificent Maha Bodhi Temple, which we see today, was built in the second century AD, and the colossal image of the Buddha was enshrined still later. It is not certain when the sacred shrine came to be called as 'Mahabodhi.' In his inscription, Asoka calls it Sambodhi. Fa-hian, who saw it in 409 AD did not mention the name. However, Hiuen Tsang, who visited it two centuries later, calls it 'Mahabodhi Vihara.' Thereafter, this name is mentioned in a number of inscriptions found at Buddha Gaya, the last one being mentioned in late 14th century.

When, Hiuen Tsang, the celebrated Chinese pilgrim, saw this Temple in 637 AD, it was at its zenith. This is how he describes the Great Temple:

> "To the East of the Bodhi tree, there is a Vihara about 160 feet or 170 feet high. Its lower foundation-wall is 20 paces or more in its face. The building (pile) is of blue tiles (bricks) covered with chunam (burnt stone lime); all the niches in the different storeys hold golden figures. The four sides of the building are covered with wonderful ornamental work; in one place figures of stringed pearls (garlands), in another figures of heavenly Rishis. The whole is surrounded by a gilded copper Amalaka fruit. The eastern face adjoins a storeyed pavillion, the projecting eaves of which rise one over the other to the height of three distinct chambers; its projecting eaves,

> its pillars, beams, doors and windows are decorated with gold and silver ornamental work, with pearls and gems let in to fill up interstices."

In the vicinity of the Maha Bodhi Vihara, Hiuen Tsang saw twenty-one stupas; the largest being the Asoka Stupa. He also saw three tanks—Buddha, Sakra and Muchalinda, and six monasteries including the biggest monastery (Sangharama) built by a king of Sri Lanka. This monastery had more than one thousand resident monks at that time.

For nearly three centuries after the visit of Hiuen Tsang, no major repairs, improvements appear to have been carried out at Buddha Gaya. It was only in 1070 AD that the first major restoration and renovation of the Maha Bodhi Vihara was undertaken by the Burmese, The last Indian Buddhist King to repair the historic Maha Bodhi Temple was Raja Asoka—balla of Siwalik Hills in the Punjab. With his aid, and that of a local chief named Purushottama Simha, several repair works were carried out in 1157 AD under the superintendence of a Buddhist monk called Dharmarakshita.

When the armed hordes of Muslims sacked Bihar in the last decade of the 12th century; destroyed Buddhist shrines and slaughtered Buddhist monks on an unprecedented scale, a considerable portion of the population fled from Buddha Gaya. According to Dharmasvamin, a Tibetan pilgrim, who visited Buddha Gaya in 1234 AD, "the place was deserted and only four monks were found staying (in the Vihara)."

Soon after Dharmasvamin's visit, the Maha Bodhi Temple was lost into oblivion. However, it appears to have been looked after by a monk for some time during the 14th century. And some repairs to the Temple were carried out by a Burmese Mission during the period 1496-1498. Thereafter, the Great Temple was deserted by the Buddhists and left unattended. Taking advantage of the situation, a Hindu Mahant, Gosain Giri occupied the Great Temple in 1590 AD. With the coming of the Mahant, the holy Buddhist shrine passed into the hands of a rival sect, and the phase of its sacrilege began.

In 1811, when Dr. Hamilton Buchanan visited Buddha Gaya, he found the Maha Bodhi Temple in utter ruins. He, however, records worship being offered to the Bodhi Tree by the Hindus, but adds that

> "Some zealous persons had lately built a stairway on the side of the terrace so that orthodox may pass without entering the porch and thus seeing the hateful image of the Buddha."

Fifty years later, in 1861, when Alexander Cunningham, the great archaeologist, visited Buddha Gaya, he was shocked to find the Mahant and his men indulging in all sorts of un-Buddhistic and offensive ceremonies in the main shrine of the Maha Bodhi Temple. By that time the Mahant had installed a Sivalingam in the middle of the sanctum, and had uprooted the Buddha image. Further, though the Mahant claimed the Maha Bodhi and the land around it as his own property yet he took no steps to repair the decaying historic temple.

In 1875, King Mindon Min of Burma, sought permission of the Government of India to repair the decaying Maha Bodhi Temple. As the repairs initiated by the Burmese were not proceeding on right lines, the then British Government undertook in 1880 the responsibility to make thorough repairs. The restoration and renovation of the Maha Bodhi Temple to its present condition, almost an exact replica of the original shrine, was a lengthy affair and cost a lot of money but the work was accomplished with rare devotion and dedication by J.D. Beglar and his team.

The Maha Bodhi Temple, as it now stands, is 170 feet high, while the base is 50 square feet. It consists of a high straight-edged pyramidal tower of nine storeys, and is surmounted by a stupa. Its entrance porch. comparatively later than the original Temple, is on the east. Each of the four sides of the tower presents several tiers of niches, while the front face has a tall lancet opening for the admission of light into the sanctum, and at the base of the tower there rises a turret at each of the four corners—a minature replica of the main spire. The main shrine room of the Temple which is situated at the ground floor is reached after passing through a vaulted passage.

The great gilded image of the Buddha enshrined in the sanctum is in the earth-touching pose (Bhumisparsa Mudra) symbolising the supreme event of Enlightenment. It is dated in the tenth century AD, and was seen by Dharmasvamin, a Tibetan pilgrim in 1234 AD. Later, it was removed by the Mahant and taken to his Math from where it was brought back by Cunningham in 1880.

Even after restoration, the property rights of the Maha Bodhi Temple and its lands continued to be vested in the Mahant. That he paid not heed to the sanctity of the shrine is evident from what Sir Edwin Arnold, the celebrated author of 'The Light of Asia' saw in 1885 when he visited Buddha Gaya. In a pathetic tone, he later wrote :

> "The Buddhist world had, indeed, well-nigh forgotten this hallowed and most interesting centre of their faith—the Mecca, the Jerusalem, of a million Oriental congregations. When I sojourned in Buddha Gaya a few years ago, I was grieved to see Maharatta peasants performing "Shraddh" in such a place, and thousands of precious ancient relics of carved stone lying in piles around."

Prompted by this stimulating description of the Seat of Buddha's Enlightenment, Anagarika Dharmapala, the first Buddhist missionary of modern times, visited Buddha Gaya on 22 January 1891, and was visibly moved by what he saw. To quote his own words:

> "The sacred Vihara—the Lord sitting on his throne and the great solemnity which pervades all round makes the heart of the pious devotee weep. How delightful! As soon as I touched with my forehead the Vajrasana a sudden impulse came to my mind. It prompted me to stop here and take care of this sacred spot—so sacred that nothing in the world is equal to this place where Prince Sakyasinha gained Enlightenment under the Bodhi Tree."

Having resolved to regain the control of Maha Bodhi Temple from the Mahant, Dharmapala decided to stay at Buddha Gaya till some satisfactory arrangements were made to preserve the sanctity of the sacred shrine. So he moved to the Burmese Rest House built in 1875. As a first step, he persuaded four Buddhist monks from Sri Lanka to come and stay at Buddha Gaya. The Bhikkhus reached Buddha Gaya in July 1891 and took up their residence in the Burmese Rest House. The Mahant objected to the presence of the Bhikkhus. And in February 1893, two of the monks were severely beaten up by his men. Two years later, in 1895, when Dharmapala attempted to install an image of the Buddha, presented to him by the people of Japan, on the upper floor of the Temple, he was assaulted and prevented by Mahant's men to do so. The Buddha image was later kept in the Burmese Rest House. The Mahant and some Hindu organisations, particularly the British India Association, London, later tried to get the Buddha image removed even from the Rest House on the plea that "it was offensive to the Hindus." But the Government did not yield.

In 1906, the Mahant filed a suit seeking ejection of the Buddhist monks from the Rest House. The Buddhists also filed a civil suit claiming control of the Maha Bodhi Temple. The legal war of nerves continued till, after independence, the Government of Bihar enacted the Bodh Gaya Temple Management Act in 1949 in accordance with which a Management Committee was constituted by the State Government in 1952 and entrusted with the management and control of the Temple, the Temple Land, and other property. As provided in the Bodh Gaya Temple Act of 1949, the Committee consists of eight members, four Hindus and four Buddhists, with the District Magistrate of Gaya as Chairman. To ensure that the Hindus have always an upper hand in the Committee, a specific provision has been made in the Act. Section 3(3) of the Act says: "District Magistrate shall be ex-officio Chairman provided that the State Government shall nominate a Hindu as Chairman of the Committee for the period during which the District Magistrate of Gaya is non-Hindu." Thus the Buddhists have practically very little say in the management of the Maha Bodhi Temple and this has adversely affected the proper preservation and development of their holy shrine.

Notwithstanding this deficiency, the Great Maha Bodhi Temple is once again a living shrine and is now visited every year by millions of pilgrims and tourists from all over the world. The prestige of this Most Sacred Buddhist Shrine has been further enhanced by the modern temples and monasteries built at Buddha Gaya by the Buddhists of Burma (Myanmar), Bhutan, China, Japan, Thailand, Tibet and others. Verily, these temples and monasteries have made Buddha Gaya an important International Centre of Buddhist Culture, Wisdom and Worship.

CONTENTS

THE ENLIGHTENED ONE

Then the Blessed One spake and said: Know, Vāseṭṭha, that from time to time a Tathāgata is born into the world, a fully Enlightened One, blessed and worthy, abounding in wisdom and goodness, happy with knowledge of the worlds, unsurpassed as a guide to erring mortals, a teacher of gods and men, a Blessed Buddha. He thoroughly understands this universe, as though he saw it face to face—the world below with all its people, the worlds above, of Mara and of Brahma—and all creatures, Samanas and Brāhmans, gods and men, and from that knowledge makes it known and teaches others. The Truth does he proclaim both in its letter and its spirit, lovely in its origin, lovely in its progress, lovely in its consummation. A higher life doth he made known in all its purity and in all its perfectness.

Tevijia Sutta

Chapter I

URUVELA—THE LAND OF ENLIGHTENMENT

Born as a prince in BC 563 at Lumbini, near Kapilavastu, the capital city of the Sakyas, Siddhartha Gautama grew up in the midst of luxury, beauty and plenty. However, slowly and slowly he was getting weary of his surroundings, and was becoming more and more contemplative. By the time he was 29, his mental make-up had crystalysed. He was anxious to find a solution to the problem of suffering which had particularly pricked his conscience on seeing an old man, a sick man and a dead man in succession while on his way to the royal park. So he decided to renounce the world forthwith, the world that was his—a kingdom, a loving wife, a newly-born son—and adopt the life of a homeless wanderer, a seeker after truth.

When Siddhartha in the prime of his youth renounced the world, and left his palace—home to seek the truth, he had no set plans. After leaving Kapilavastu, the Prince turned mendicant trekked on foot a distance of 650 kilometres and reached Rajagaha (modern Rajgir in Bihar), the capital of Magadha, which was then known as the abode of great philosophers and leaders of thought.

Entering the city gate in the morning, the Bodhisatta* went from house to house begging for his alms. His charming personality, dignity and splendid beauty caught the imagination of the people. "So charming and well-groomed," they said "that he does not seem at all like a mendicant." Soon his arrival in the city became a talk of the town, and reached the ears of King Bimbisara, who had in the meanwhile come to know of the dramatic renunciation of Siddhartha, the son of his friend King Suddhodana. Curious to find the truth, Bimbisara went out himself

* Pali, Bodhisatta; Sanskrit, Bodhisattva.

truth, Bimbisara went out himself to look for the Prince. In the meanwhile, the Bodhisatta had begged sufficient food and retired to the foot of the Pandava hill to take the food in his bowl. Hardly he had finished his meal that King Bimbisara reached the Pandava hill, and addressed the Bodhisatta in these words:

> "When I consider thy race, beginning with the sun, thy fresh youth, and thy conspicuous beauty, I wonder whence comes this resolve of thine, so out of all harmony with the rest, set wholly on a mendicant's life, not on a kingdom? Thy limbs are worthy of red sandalwood perfumes—they do not deserve the rough contact of red cloth, this hand of thine is fit to protect subjects, it deserves not to hold food given by another. If, therefore, gentle youth, thou desire not thy paternal kingdom, then in thy generosity, accept forthwith, one half of my kingdom." (Buddhacarita of Asvaghosha, Canto x, vv. 23-25).

The Bodhisatta politely declined the offer[1] so graciously made by the Magadha King. Convinced of his determination to follow the path he had chosen, Bimbisara begged the Bodhisatta to pay his first visit to him as soon as he had attained enlightenment and found the truth. This the Bodhisatta promised to do.

At Rajagaha, the Bodhisatta first went to the ashram of Alara Kalama, and within a short time, he mastered all what he was taught. Not satisfied, he went further to the ashram of Uddaka Ramaputta and trained himself in the ways of meditation as taught by that great teacher. But he was still not satisfied. Therefore, the Bodhisatta marched forward towards the forest of Uruvela[2] (Uruvilva), near Gaya, to practise asceticism, and find the truth himself. The Bodhisatta's first halt in the forest of Uruvela was on the Gayasirsa Hill where he meditated for some time. Then, he moved on to the outskirts of the village of Uruvela or Uruvilva (modern Urel) on the eastern bank of river Neranjara,[3] and found the place congenial for ascetic practices. The five parivrajakas whom the Bodhisatta had met at Rajagaha, also joined him there. Together they started practising asceticism in the lovely land of Uruvela.

Describing the Bodhisatta's arrival at Uruvela, the Lalitavistara (Ed. R.L. Mitra, p. 311) says[4]:

> "Pleasantly picturesque is this part of land. Delightful is the sight of the grassy woodland. The river (Neranjara) is flowing on in a glassy stream, showing the bathing places with

gradual descents of steps presenting a charming landscape, and affording glimpses into the neighbouring hamlets easy of access. This must needs be the fitting place for a scion of a noble race strenuously striving after the highest attainments!" Forthwith Siddhartha, the eternal glory of the Sakya race, made up his mind to enter on his epoch-making struggle on the very site."

For six years, the Bodhisatta practised extreme austerities and self-mortification. Not only he tormented and tortured his body, he also lived on very scanty food; sometimes he lived on wild roots and fruits, or on windfalls only. Consequently, his body had been reduced to a mere skeleton. Later, the Buddha himself told his pitiable condition at that time in these words:

> "My body became extremely lean. The bones of my backbone were bent like a row of spindles. As the beams of an old bamboo shed stick out, so did my ribs stick out. My body was as if a living skeleton. When I thought I would touch the skin of my stomach, I actually caught my backbone, and when I thought I would touch my backbone, I took hold of the skin of my stomach, so much did the skin of my stomach cling to my backbone. To give relief to my body I stroked my limbs with my hand. And as I did so, the decayed hairs fell from my body. . . ." (Maha Saccaka Sutta, 36, Majjhima Nikaya).

Such was the condition of Gautama at the end of six long painful years of extreme mortification of the self. Then one day he fell uncon-cious, and was found by a shepherd who gave him milk and took him into his care. By and by the Bodhisatta regained strength and beauty which had been lost due to excessive austerities. Realising the futility of the mortification of flesh, he began taking solid food. Annoyed with him on partaking of food, his five companions left him. Thus the Buddha-to-be was left alone to pursue his path.

Determined to achieve enlightenment; to know the ultimate truth, the Bodhisatta now concentrated more on meditative practises and less on austerities. At that time there lived in the neighbourhood a woman named Sujata, daughter of the chief of the village Senani.[5] She was expecting a baby and had vowed that if a son was born to her she would make a special food offering to the deity of a nearby banyan tree. Sujata's vow was fulfilled; she was blessed with a son. So she prepared a special rice-pudding (*kheer*), and sent her maid to the banyan tree to make necessary arrangements. Meanwhile, the Bodhisatta while wandering had come that way and sat down under that banyan tree to meditate. When the maid came, she was astonished to see an illustrious figure sitting under the tree. She rushed back to tell her mistress that the deity himself had appeared to accept the offering. The grateful Sujata excitedly hurried to the banyan tree, and offered to Bodhisatta the specially prepared rice-pudding in a golden bowl. Sujata was so overwhelmed by the personality of the Buddha-to-be that she reverentially saluted him and withdrew, leaving the precious bowl behind.

After taking the food, the future Buddha came to the Neranjara river, and putting the bowl in the water, he said: "If I am to attain enlightenment, may this golden bowl swim upstream; if not, let it go down." The vessel, indeed, began to float against the current, and at last sank.

Then crossing the river, the Bodhisatta came to the Bodhi tree on its western bank. On the way a grasscutter gave him some 'kusa grass,' a soft pliable grass of which mats are made of. Having spread the grass at the foot of the shady Pippal tree, the future Buddha turned to face the East, and sat cross-legged at Earth's centre, and vowed to himself:

> "Blood may dry up, flesh may decay, bones may fall apart, but I will not leave this place until I attain enlightenment."
>
> (Mahaniddesa, p. 476 Pali Text Society)

With such determination to attain Sambodhi, he sat there pondering deep and deep into the mysteries of life. And on that fateful day when he was about to attain Buddhahood, the Mara, the celebrated Lord of Evil Thoughts and Evil Passions, swung into action and attempted in various ways to thwart his efforts. First of all, the Evil One, tried to tempt him with sensual pleasures through his daughters but they failed to attract the attention of the Bodhisatta. When the Mara found that the Bodhisatta was determined to pursue his path, he, in frustration, assaulted him with weapons of darkness, thunder and lightning, storms and hurricanes, and sent blast after blast of wind at such velocity as to uproot the forest itself. But all this had no effect on the future Buddha. He remained steadfast on his seat. Looking at the bawildered Mara, he stretched his right hand towards the ground, and said: "May this earth be my witness that I will attain enlightenment and put an end to the sorrows of mankind." Then the earth shook; a great noise arose, and there burst in the sky a thunder-bolt making a roaring noise which fell in mid-air. Terrified, Mara's army ran helter-skelter. Having failed to recover the throne to which he had laid claim, Mara disappeared discomforted. The gods celebrated the Buddha's victory; so night fell.

Then entering into deeper contemplation, the Buddha during the first watch of that wonderful night acquired the knowledge of his past lives in various planes of existence; in the second watch he acquired the supernormal divine vision; in the third watch he fathomed the law of cause and effect and gained insight into the destruction of mental cankers; and at sunrise he attained Supreme Enlightenment, Omniscience.

Thus on the fullmoon day of Vaisakha in BC 528, Gautama became a Buddha, the Awakened One. The Buddha later also came to be known as Sammasambuddha—the Perfectly Enlightened One, Bhagava—the Blessed One, Tathagata—the Perfect One, Sugata—the Happy One or the Accomplished One, and Sakyamuni—the Sage of the Sakyas. The tree under which he sat became known as the Bodhi Tree, and the area as Bodh Gaya or Buddha Gaya.

The Seat[6] of Buddha's Enlightenment is 12 kilometres to the south of Gaya in Bihar, and there stands on the site the Great Maha Bodhi Temple, the most sacred shrine venerated by the Buddhists through the ages. The sacred Bodhi Tree is to the west of the Maha Bodhi Temple, and the spot sitting where the Buddha attained Supreme Enlightenment, Sambodhi, is now marked by the Vajrasana, the Diamond Throne seen between the Bodhi Tree and the Temple.

Gautama Buddha, after His enlightenment, continued to sit for a week at the foot of the Bodhi Tree enjoying the bliss of Nirvana. He spent the second week in walking to and fro near the Bodhi tree. The third week He spent standing nearby gazing at the Bodhi tree, out of gratitude for giving him shelter. He spent the fourth week in meditation near the Bodhi tree. He spent the fifth week under the Ajapala Nyagrodha tree where Sujata had offered him a meal of rice-pudding. He spent the sixth week near the Muchalinda lake where Muchalinda, the Naga King of the lake, is said to have sheltered the Buddha from rain. The Buddha spent the seventh week at the foot of the Rajyatana tree. Here He was offered cakes of barley and honey as food by two merchants, Tapassu and Bhallika, from Utkala, modern Orissa, who per chance had come there in the course of their travelling.

From the Rajyatana tree, the Buddha returned to the Bodh Tree. Then, He reverently bowed to the sacred Bo-tree, and thoughfully proceeded to Isipatana, modern Sarnath, near Varanasi in Uttar Pradesh. There, the Blessed One delivered His First Sermon and set in motion the Wheel of the Dhamma, the event that constituted the beginning of the Holy Spiritual and Cultural Empire of Buddhism.

NOTES

1. In the Prabhabha Sutta the account given by the Buddha Himself is as follows:

   > "Having sat down the king then exchanged the usual ceremonious greetings with him, and after the complimentary talk he spoke these words: (418) Thou art both young and delicate, a lad in his first youth, possessed of a fine complexion, like a high-born Khattiya. (419)
   >
   > I will ornament the army-house, and at the head of the assembly of chiefs (naga) give thee wealth; enjoy it and tell me thy birth, when asked." (420)

   The *Sutta-Nipata*, translated from Pali by V. Fausboll, The Sacred Books of the East, Part I, (1881, reprint Delhi, 1973, p. 68.)

2. According to Buddhaghosha and Dhammapala, the two great Pali scholars, the name Uruvela signifies either a great expanse of sandy tract or sandy banks formed by deposits of sediments due to the over flooding of the stream. (Papanca Sudani (Siamese Edn., Pt. II), p. 232 and Udana Commentary (Siamese Edn.), p. 32.

   (For a detailed discussion on Uruvela, See B.M. Barua, Gaya and Buddha Gaya, 1934 reprint, Delhi, 1975), pp. 99. 102).

3. In the wide range of Buddhist literature, as a matter of fact, Uruvela is found invariably associated with the river Neranjara or Nairanjana (modern Nilajan or Lilajan). From this it may be easily deducted that the tract of Uruvela was mainly washed by the Neranjara, and not by the Phalgu. The Vinaya-Mahavagga (p. 33) plainly indicates a northward course of the Neranjara so that any thing swept by the current of the stream might be clearly visible to the people at Nadi and at Gaya proper in its onward flow. We may gather from this that the Phalgu and the stream further north were somehow just the continuation of the Neranjara. *Vinaya-Mahavagga*, p. I, *Udana*, p. 10, *Uruvellyam viharati najja Neranjaraya fire. Lalita-vistara*, Mitra's Edn., p. 311: *yenoruvilai.... tatrddrakshin nad'm Nairnnjandam. Mahavastu*, Vol. II, p. 123). (Cf. B.M. Barua, Gaya and Buddha Gaya, Book I, 1975, p. 102.)

4. The text in Lalitavistara (Ed., Mitra, Calcutta, 1896, p. 311) is as follows:

   > *"Ramaṇiyo vata bho bhūmibhāgo, pāsādiko cha vanasaṇḍo, nadī cha sandati setakā sūpatitthā ramaniyā samantā cha gocharagāmo, alam vat 'idam kulaputtasa padhānatthikassa padhānāyati."*

5. The principal locality in Uruvela of the Buddha's time was Sen-nigama or Senani-gama, corresponding to the Senapatigrama of the Sanskrit Buddhist works (*Lalitavistara*, p. 311; *Mahavastu*, Vol II, p. 123). In commenting on the name of this locality, Buddhaghosha points out that in a remote period of time it served as a military outpost or cantonment. (Papancasudani, Siamese Ed., Part II, p. 223).

6. "The original seat of Sakyamuni under the Pipal at Gaya, where all past Buddhas—have reached perfect Enlightenment, and all future Buddhas will reach, is called by Hiuen Tsang Vajrasana, Diamond Seat. It was in his time protected by brickwork. . . . The Bodhimanda, or Narasimhasana, is held to be the centre of the earth."

(H. Kern, Manual of Indian Buddhism (1898, reprint, Delhi, 1974, p. 97).

Asvaghosha in his Buddhacarita says: "This is the navel of earth's surface, entirely possessed of the highest power; for there is no other spot on earth which can bear the force of his (Bodhisatta's) concentrated thought."

(The *Buddhacarita*, trans, E.H. Johnston, 1936, reprint, Delhi, 1972, p. 201.)

Chapter II

ASOKA AND BUDDHA GAYA

For nearly two centuries after the Mahaparinirvana of the Buddha in BC 483, Buddhism survived as a small religious community but it was well-entrenched in Magadha and many other adjoining areas. Then came Asoka, the third Mauryan Emperor (273 BC — 232 BC), who transformed Buddhism from an obscure faith to a world religion.

Asoka had inherited a well-established and well-organised Empire, extending from Mysore to Afghanistan, founded by his grandfather, Chandragupta Maurya and maintained intact by his father, Bindusara. To this vast Empire, Asoka added Kalinga (modern Orissa) which he conquered after a bloody war in BC 261. This war completely ruined Kalinga as in it thousands of people were killed and injured. The large scale destruction in the Kalinga War deeply influenced the mind of Asoka, and it brought a revolution in his character. With this event, his outlook, both in his personal and public life, changed. Consequently, he sought solace in the sublime teachings of the Buddha, and declared that henceforth he would follow the Buddha-Dhamma in all his actions — spiritual as well as temporal. "The chiefest conquest is not Rajya-Vijaya but Dhamma Vijaya," he said. As such, he decided to launch a vigorous campaign to preach and propagate the message of the Buddha, the Lord of Mercy and Compassion.

However, before launching his 'Dhamma-Vijaya' campaign, Asoka, the first great royal patron of Buddhism, visited the Holy Seat of Buddha's Enlightenment, and worshipped in person the sacred Bodhi Tree. Asoka was so much enchanted by the serene and peaceful environment around the sacred Bodhi Tree that he decided then and there to discard forthwith hunting and pleasure trips, passionate pastime of the kings and princes at that time, and, instead to undertake 'Pilgrimages of Piety,' dhamma-yatras, at regular intervals and propagate the Dhamma among the people. In the Major Rock Edict VIII, Asoka says, "Now, king Priyadarsi, Beloved of the Gods, visited Sambodhi ten years after his coronation. Thence started these pilgrimages of piety." During these *dhamma-yatras*, Asoka made gifts to the poor and the needy, contacted the people of the countryside, instructed them in Dhamma, and discussed with them the principles of Dhamma. All this enhanced the prestige and popularity of the Dhamma.

Asoka visited Sambodhi, as he preferred to call the place, more than once. And the memory of one of his visit to the Bodhi Tree has been preserved for us in a first century BC sculpture on the East Gateway, front side, bottom architrave of the Great Sanchi Stupa in Madhya Pradesh. The representation at Sanchi shows the branches of the Bodhi Tree rising above a barrel-vaulted temple enshrining *triratana*, and Asoka supported by two queens. The sculpture shows a circular/pillard structure with open sides enclosing the Bodhi Tree with *Vajrasana* at its base. Asoka is seen twice here. Once descending from the elephant and the second time proceeding towards the Bodhi tree with clasped hands.

Asoka's visit to Sambodhi or Buddha Gaya, alongwith his spiritual preceptor, Upagupta (Moggaliputta Tissa) is described at length in the *Asokavadana*, an ancient Sanskrit text. Identifying the sites associated with the Blessed One at Buddha Gaya, Upagupta tells the Emperor in these words:

"In this place, the Bodhisattva practised self-mortification for six years."

And he added:

For six long years, the great Sage
undertook fierce austerities,
and then gave them up realizing
this was not the way to highest knowledge.

"In this place, Nanda and Nandabala, the daughters[1] of a village headman, offered to Bodhisattva sweetened milk-rice which had been condensed sixteen times."

And he added:

Here the most eloquent Great Hero

1 Apparently these two daughters are the same as Sujata, who is usually portrayed as the one offering the milk-rice.

enjoyed Nanda's sweetened milk-rice,
and then set out
for the seat of enlightenment.

"In this place, the Bodhisattva, on his way to the Bodhi tree, was praised by the naga King, Kalika."

And he added:

Coming along this path toward the seat of enlightenment
where he sought immortality,
the most eloquent of men was praised
by Kalika, chief of serpents.

Then Asoka fell at the elder Upagupta's feet, and making an *anjali*, he said:

I would like to meet the naga king
who saw the Tathagata
walking along this path
as unstoppable as an elephant bull in rut.

And immediately, Kalika the naga king appeared before

Upagupta and said, making as *anjali*, "Elder, what is your command?"

Upagupta said to King Asoka: "This, your majesty, is Kalika, the naga king who praised the Blessed One while he was heading along this path towards the Bodhi tree."

Asoka said to the naga, making an *anjali*:

You saw my pearless Master,
his complexion like blazing gold
and his face like the autumn moon.
Recount for me some of the Buddha's qualities;
tell me what it was like—the splendour of the Sugata

"I am unable fully to describe it in words," replied Kalika, "but, in brief, listen:

Beneath his feet, the whole earth
and its mountain range trembled
in six different ways.
The Sugata shone on the world of men
like a beautiful never-waning moon,
surpassing the sun in splendour."

Now when the king had built a caitya at that spot, the elder Upagupta led him to the foot of The Bodhi tree, stretched out his right hand and said: "In this place, great king, the Bodhisattva first defeated the forces of Mara with the power of his loving kindness, and then completely realized total unsurpassed enlightenment."

And he added :

Here at the seat of enlightenment
the greatest of sages dispersed
and quickly repelled the forces of Namuci (Mara)
And here that peerless individual
attained everlasting, exalted,
supreme enlightenment.

And hearing this the king made an offering of one hundred thousand pieces of gold to the Bodhi Tree and built a caitya there.

They went on, and after a while the elder Upagupta stopped and said to Asoka: "In this place, the Blessed One received from the celestial guardians of the four quarters four stone begging bowls which he joined into a single bowl. Over here, the merchants Trapusu and Bhallika made him an offering of alms food. And here the Blessed One, on his way to Benares, was praised by the Ajivika Upata."

(John S. Strong, The Legend of King Asoka, A Study and Translation of the *Asokavadana*, Princeton, New Jersey, U.S.A. 1983, pp. 248-250).

Asoka's encounter with the naga king is told even in a more dramatic manner in a Sri Lankan chronicler, *Mahavamsa.* One day, we are told Asoka meets the naga king Mahakala (Kalika), and when he had brought him and made him sit down upon the throne under the white canopy, when he had done homage to him with gifts of various flowers, and had bidden the sixteen thousand women of the palace to surround him, the king spoke thus: "Let us behold the bodily form of the omniscient Great Sage, of Him who hath the boundless knowledge, who hath set rolling the wheel of the true doctrine. The naga king created a beauteous figure of the Buddha, endowed with the thirty-two greater signs and brilliant with the eighty lesser signs of a Buddha, surrounded by the fathom long rays of glory and adorned with the crown of flames. At the sight thereof the king was filled with joy and amazement. (Geiger, tr., pp. 33-34)

Asoka was so much devoted and attached to the Bodhi Tree, sitting under which the Buddha had attained Enlightenment, that his excessive zeal even earned the wrath of one of his queens. After the demise of his chief queen, Asandhimita, who had been his faithful companion for many years, Asoka married Tissarakkha or Tishyarakshita. The new queen turned out to be a vain woman. She is said to have been so much irritated by Asoka's devotion to the Dhamma that she attempted to destroy the holy tree at Buddha Gaya by hiring a sorceress adept in black magic. As the Bodhi Tree began to wither, Asoka was so much upset that he declared with some emotion: "If the tree of the Lord comes to die, I too shall surely expire."

Fortunately for Asoka, this did not happen. Tissarakkha soon came to realize her error and asked the sorceress to undo the spell. This she did in time, and the Bodhi Tree bloomed again to the delight of all.

Asoka had not only lavished gifts on the sacred Bodhi Tree but had also built the first chaitya (temple) at Buddha Gaya. A portrayal of the Asokan temple has been found in a second century BC bas-relief discovered at the Bharhut Stupa in Madhya Pradesh. The *Asokavadana* also records this fact. And Hiuen Tsang, the celebrated Chinese pilgrim, who visited Buddha Gaya in AD 637, also records that the first temple at this sacred spot was built by Asoka-raja. So the development of Buddha Gaya as a holy shrine began with Asoka.

Chapter III

WHEN AND BY WHOM THE TEMPLE WAS BUILT ?

The first temple on the sacred spot sitting where Gautama had gained Sambodhi, supreme enlightenment, and become a Buddha was built by Asoka, the First Buddhist Emperor of India (BC 273-232). That Asoka had indeed built such a temple or chaitya at Buddha Gaya is confirmed atleast by three independent sources:

(a) A portrayal of the Asokan temple built at Bodh Gaya in about BC 250 has been found in an inscribed *bas-relief* at the Bharhut Stupa in Madhya Pradesh. The *bas-relief* shows the Bodhi Tree with the Vajrasana (Diamond Throne) in front adorned with umbrella and garlands, and sheltered by a pillard-hall. It also shows a railing around the Bodhi Tree, with a gate on the east. Since the Bharhut Stupa belongs to the period BC 120-100, it can be safely assumed that the artist has presented here a reasonably realistic picture of the temple built by Asoka.

(b) Hiuen Tsang, the second Chinese pilgrim, who visited the shrine in AD 637, recording a tradition, says:
"Asoka-raja had built a small temple at Bodh Gaya." A Burmese inscription dated in the eleventh century also says that "this is one of the 84,000 shrines erected by the great king Dhamma Asoka."

(c) Among the few remnants of the Asokan temple, discovered by Cunningham, were the polished sandstone throne and two pillar-bases *in situ*, "one on each side of the sandstone throne, at equal distances from ends." The bases showed that each of the two pillars had an octagonal shaft above a pedestal with a pot or vase ornament at the top of a gradation of steps. The southern base was hidden under the southern wall of the chamber, "while the northern one was quite clear of the southern wall." A third pillar-base was also discovered, but not actually *in situ*. Having regard to the antiquity and location of these pillars, "and comparing them with the view of the Asoka's Temple, preserved in the bas-relief of Bharhut," Cunningham concluded "that we have found some of the actual remains of the original building."

Nearly two centuries after Asoka, a carved stone-railing enclosing the Bodhi Tree was put up by the Noble Lady Kurangi, Nagadevi and Sirima. The remains of this railing still survive, and so are the brief inscriptions left behind by these pious ladies. (For details, please see notes.)

Later, the Asokan Temple was dismantled, and the magnificent Maha Bodhi Temple that we see today was built. However, who built this temple and when is shrouded in mystery.

Much of the confusion about the date of the Maha Bodhi Temple has been created by the writings of the Chinese pilgrims, Fa-hian and Hiuen Tsang. Fa-hian, the first Chinese pilgrim who saw it in AD 409 does not specifically mention the name. The second Chinese pilgrim, Hiuen Tsang, who visited Buddha Gaya 230 years later in AD 637, calls it 'Mahabodhi Vihara' and gives a detailed account of its construction. According to him:

> "On the site of the present vihara, Asoka-raja at first built a small vihara. Afterwards, there was a Brahman who reconstructed it on a larger scale. At first, this Brahman was not a believer in the law of the Buddha, and sacrificed to Mahesvara. Having heard that this heavenly spirit (god) dwelt in the Snowy Mountains, he forthwith went there with his younger brother to seek by prayer (his wishes). The Deva said, "Those who pray should aim to acquire some extensive religious merit. If you who pray have not this ground (of merit), then neither can I grant what you pray for."
>
> The Brahman said, "What meritorious work can I set about to enable me to obtain my desire?"
>
> The god said, "If you wish to plant a superior root (growth) of merit, then seek a superior field (in which to acquire it). The Bodhi Tree is the place for attaining the fruit of a Buddha. You should straightway return there, and by the Bodhi Tree erect a large

vihara, and excavate a large tank, and devote all kinds of religious offerings (to the service). You will then surely obtain your wishes."

The Brahman having received the divine communication, conceived a believing heart, and they both returned to the place. The elder built the vihara, the younger excavated the tank, and then they prepared large religious offerings, and sought with diligence their heart's desire (vow). The result followed at once. The Brahman became the great minister of the king. He devoted all his emoluments to the work of charity." (Beal, Buddhist Records of the Western World, II:119-120.)

The story told by Hiuen Tsang is incomplete and unconvincing. It is difficult to believe it as the sources needed to construct such a large magnificent Temple would only be available to a king.

A fourteenth century Burmese inscription discovered at Buddha Gaya gives yet another twist to the history of the construction of the Maha Bodhi Temple. According to it, the original Temple was erected by the great king Dhamma Asoka. "In lapse of time, having fallen into disrepair, it was rebuilt by a priest named Naik-Mahanta. Again, being ruined, it was restored by Raja Sado Mang. After a long interval it was once more demolished, when Raja Sempyu-sakhen-tra-Mengi appointed his guru, Sri Dharma Raja Guna, to superintend the building. He proceeded to the spot with his disciple, Sri Kasyapa, but they were unable to complete it, although aided in every way by the Raja. Afterwards Varadasi-naik-thera petitioned the Raja to undertake it, which he readily assented, commissioning Prince Pyutasing to the work, who again deputed the younger Pyusakheng, and his minister, Ratha, to cross over and repair the sacred building. It was thus constructed a fourth time, and finished on Friday the 10th day of Pyadola, in the Sakkaraj year 667 (AD 1305). On Sunday, the 8th of Tachhanmungla, 668 (AD 1306), it was consecrated with splendid ceremonies and offerings. (Cunningham, Mahabodhi: 76-77)

In view of the conflicting reports by the Chinese pilgrims, and the Burmese inscription cited above, there is a wide difference of opinion among the modern scholars in regard to the date of the Great Maha Bodhi Temple. Just to quote three of them:

(i) According to Rajendra Lal Mitra (Buddha Gaya: 1878) "The Gupta inscription . . . , though not referring to the erection of the temple forcibly impress the idea that the temple must have been existing in the second century, and we must, therefore.

proceed to the first for the age of the monument, and that may be looked upon as the terminus *ad quem*. Mitra concludes: "It may be safely accepted as facts that the spot on which the Great Temple now stands was once the site of some structure, not a chaitya, which had been built by Asoka, and that the old monument was for some cause or other removed to make room for the temple. If we allow 150 years for the duration of Asoka's monument, we have the beginning of the first century BC to be the terminus a *qus* for the present," and, "so far the chain of evidence may be accepted to be tolerably complete, or as much so as we can reasonably expect in a case of this kind, though some of the links are not quite so strong as could be wished. This gives us a period of two hundred years, from the beginning of the first century BC to the close of the first century AC within which we must look for the date of the Great Temple of Buddha Gaya."

(ii) Alexander Cunningham (Mahabodhi: 1892) assigns the construction of the Temple to the period between AD 120-160, and

(iii) Benimadhab Barua (Gaya and Buddha Gaya: 1934) opines that "the great temple may have come into existence sometime after the visit of Fa Hian and decidedly before the coming of Hiuen Tsang, i.e., sometime between the 5th and the 7th century A.D."

Let us first of all consider the view expressed by B.M. Barua. In suggesting that the Great Temple may have come into existence after the visit of Fa-hian in AD 409, he has assumed that the first Chinese pilgrim had not seen the Temple and that he does not describe it in his travel account. But the very premise of assuming 'omission' by Fa-hian is not well-founded, rather it is incorrect.

Fa-hian was a man of few words, and his description of Buddha Gaya is very sketchy. For instance, he says "Where Buddha attained to Buddhahood, there are three monasteries, each with resident priests." He neither names the monasteries nor gives any details thereof. He does not even mention by name the grand monastery built by the King of Sri Lanka only a few decades before his visit in 409 AD. And to know what sort of this monastery was, we have to turn to Hiuen Tsang, the second Chinese pilgrim, who visited Buddha Gaya in 637 AD. According to him, "the Mahabodhi sangharama built by a former King of Sri Lanka "had six halls, with towers of observation of three storeys; was surrounded by a wall of defence 30 or 40 feet high, and its ornamentation was in the richest colours. The statue of Buddha was cast in gold and silver, decorated with gems and precious stones. The stupas were high and large in proportion, and beautifully ornamented.'' (Beal, Buddhist Records, II: 133). Since Fa-hian takes no notice of such a grand edifice and does not specifically names it, can we say that the Sri Lankan Monastery did not exist at the time of his visit. To think so, would be a folly.

Similarly, though Fa-hian has not specifically named the Great Maha Bodhi Temple yet the Temple was very much there, and he had seen it. He has even covered it under the description of ''four great pagodas handed down by unbroken tradition, namely, on the spot where the Buddha was born, where he became a Lo-han (Buddha), where he preached the Faith, and where he passed away.'' (Giles, The Travels of Fa-hien : 55).

Hence, B.M. Barua's suggestion that the Maha Bodhi Temple was built after Fa-hian's visit in AD 409 is not tenable. In particular, his suggestion that the Temple may have been built in the sixth century AD during the reign of king Sasanka is ridiculous and deserves outright rejection.

R.L. Mitra's view that the Great Temple may have been built sometime between the first century BC and the first century AC is also not correct. It is rather on the lower side, though his upper limit, first century AD, is not far off from the actual period of construction of the Mahavihara.

According to Cunningham, the present magnificent Maha Bodhi Temple was built in the second century AD. As it was built over the remains of the Asoka's temple, the Vajrasana Throne retains its original position of Buddha's Seat of Enlightenment. The age of the present Temple is testified by the presence of a gold coin of King Huvishka amongst the relics found in front of the inner Throne, alongwith some punch-marked silver coins.

In 1871, Cunningham found three distinct layers in the flooring of the main chamber of the Temple on the ground floor; the upper layer being represented by a granite pavement, the middle layer by a pavement of sandstone, and the lower layer by a plaster floor. Inside this chamber, he found a basalt throne of which the blue stone facing stood on the granite pavement. Removing this plaster facing of the second throne he discovered a ball of stiff earth or clay, which on being broken yielded the relics

Cunningham says:

On removing the plaster facing of the inner Vajrasana Throne there was discovered in the middle of the front face, and just below the sandstone floor, and resting on the upper plastered floor, a ball of stiff earth or clay, which on being broken yielded the following relics:

Gold— 2 impressions in thin gold on the obverse face of a gold coin of Huvishka joined together, and held by a ring.

1 Crescent of thin gold, 0.6 inch broad.

4 Flowers, 0.75 inch, with a pale sapphire in centre of each.

3 Shells, 0.6 inch long.

4 Kamarak fruits, 0.2 inch broad.

5 Buttons, or knobs, 0.45 inch broad.

26 large discs, 37.5 grains, or 1.44 each.

29 small discs, 11 grains, 0.38 each.

Silver — 5 punch-marked coils, one with human figures, besides many small shapeless fragments.

1 thing hemisphere.

27 large discs.

14 small discs.

Gems — 145 Pearls, small, all back with age. Coral, pale; about 3 Table spoons of bits and several coral shell ornaments.

Crystal, numerous fragments, all uncut. Sapphires, small fragments, valueless. Rubies, small fragments, valueless. Emeralds, small fragments, valueless.

Afterwards it was found, on minute examination, that all the remains of plaster taken off the Sandstone Throne contained small fragments of pounded coral, sapphire, crystal, pearl & c., of which as much as a basket full was collected. In fact, the mortar, instead of being composed of sand lime, consisted of coarsely pounded coral mixed with small fragments of sapphire, crystal, pearl, and ivory, bound together with lime.'' (Mahabodhi: 20)

He says further:

"The early date of this deposit is attested by the presence of the five-punch-marked silver coins, which would point to a date as early as the 2nd or 3rd century A.D.; when these coins were still current. The gold impressions also of Huvishka's coin would seem to point to the period of his reign as the actual time when the deposit was made, or about 120 to 160 AD."

Cunningham adds:

Another corroboration of this date is derived from an inscription on the pedestal of a statue of Buddha which was found near a small ruined Temple close to the South gate of the Railing of the Great Temple. The early date of this statue is attested by the unmistakable Indo-Scythian or Gupta style of the letters and sculptures; but as the inscription is dated in the Samvat year 64, and the record is worded in the usual form of the Indo-Scythian inscriptions found at Mathura, I have no doubt that it belongs to the 2nd century of the Christian era. In another place I have given my reasons for reckoning the dates of Indo-Scythian inscriptions by the Seleukidan era, by omitting the hundreds. In the present case the date of 64 would represent 464 of the Seleukidan era, equivalent to 152 AD,[1] which, as it agrees with the ascertained dates of Huvishka's reign, may be accepted as the actual date of the building of the Temple in which the statue was enshrined." (Mahabodhi: 21)

Sir Alexander Cunningham was the first Director General of the Archaeological Survey of India. He was intimately associated with the excavations in and around the Buddha Gaya Temple, and had examined minutely each and every sculpture, every stone, and every pebble lying scattered around the Temple during his half a dozen visits in 1861, 1862, 1871, 1875, 1876, and 1880. He was also a keen observer and interpreter of the archaeological remains. Hence, his view that the Great Maha Bodhi Temple must have been built in the second century AD during the reign of King Huvishka appears to be realistic and reliable. Not only that, the Temple may have been even built with liberal support from Huvishka. Of course, the Great Maha Bodhi Temple was extensively repaired, renovated and embellished in the following centuries by the devout Buddhists from India and abroad, and the present Temple is the result of the labour of many, many generations.

1 If the date be referred to the Saka Samvat, then the year 64 added to 78 AD will give AD 142 as the date of the statue.

NOTES

1. There are as many as fifteen brief Inscriptions of Kurangi on the pillars of the Old Stone-Railing. Their contents are as follows:

Text

Ayāye Kuraṃgiye dānaṃ (.)

Translation

The gift of the Noble Lady Kurangi

Text

Ayāye Kuraṃgiye dinam (.)

Translation

Donated by the Noble Lady Kurangi

2. Two Coping inscriptions of Kurangi and Sirima are as follows:

Text

(*Rāño Kosi*) *ki-putrāsa Iṃdagimitrāsa pājāvatiye jivā-putrāye Kuraṃgiye dānaṃ* (:) *rājā-pāsādā-cetikā-(Siri) mā(ye)* (*dinam*).

Text

(*Rāño Ko*) *siki-putrasa Iṃdagimitrasa pajavatiye jivā-putrāya Kuraṃgiye dinam* (:) *rājā-pāsādā-cetikā Si* (*rimāya dānaṃ.*)

Translation

The gift of Kurangi, the wife of King Indragnimitra, — (Kurangi who is) the mother of living sons: (the gift as well) of Sirima (Srimati), a female donor from the (monastic abode)

—"Indragnimitra's palace."

3. The inscription of Sirima on a mutilated pillar of the Old Stone-Railing is as follows:

Text

Rāño Iṃ(*dāgimitrā*) (....) (*S*) *irimāye* — (.)

Rāño Imdagimitrā

(*sa prāsādu-cetika-*) *Sirimaye* (*dānaṃ*)

Translation

"(The gift) of Sirima, a female donor from the Indragnimitra-prasada.

4. The Inscription of Nagadevi on a pillar of the Old Stone-Railing is as follows:

Text

Rāño Brahmamitrasa pājāvātiye Nagadevaye dānaṃ (.)

Translation

The gift of Nagadevi, the wife of King Brahmamitra.

(B.M. Barua, Gaya and Buddha Gaya: 66-69);

(Cunningham, Mahabodhi: 15)

Chapter IV

SRI LANKAN MONKS AND MONASTERY

Buddhism was introduced into Sri Lanka in the third century BC by Venerable Mahinda, the son of Asoka the Great. The King of Sri Lanka, Devanampiya Tissa, not only himself accepted the Dhamma but exhorted his subjects also to do the same. No wonder, the Buddha-Dhamma soon became popular, and many sons of the soil came forward to don the yellow robes of monks. When some women expressed desire to join the Sangha, the king of Sri Lanka, as suggested by *thera* Mahinda, requested Asoka to send *theri* Sanghamitta and some other nuns to ordain the women of Sri Lanka. He also requested Asoka to send a sapling of the sacred Bodhi Tree to be planted in his capital as an inspiring symbol of the Buddha. This message was sent by the king Devanampiya Tissa through Arittha, his nephew and his minister. *Mahavamsa* (Chapter XVIII) tells us :

> "The ruler of the land meditating on the proposition of the *thera*, of bringing over the great Bo-tree as well as the *theri* Sanghamitta ; on a certain day, within the term of that vassa, seated in his place by the side of the *thera* consulted his ministers, himself sent for and advised with his maternal nephew the minister Arittha. Having selected him for that mission, the king addressed this question to him. "My child art thou able repairing to the court of Dhammasoka, to escort hither the great Bo-tree and the *theri* Sanghamitta?" "Gracious lord, I am able to bring these from thence hither; provided, on my return to this land, I am permitted to enter into the priesthood." The monarch replying, "Be it so" — deputed him thither. He, taking charge of this message both the thera and of the sovereign, respectfully took his leave. And departing on the second day of the increasing moon of the month

"assayuja" embarked at Jambukolapattana. By the power of the *thera's* will traversing the ocean, he reached the delightful city of Pupphapura on the very day of his departure."

How, after consultations with his spiritual guide, Ven. Moggaliputta Tissa, Asoka decided to accede to both the requests of the king of Sri Lanka, and made arrangements to cut a branch of the southern part of the sacred Bo-Tree is narrated in the same Chapter of *Mahavamsa* like this:

"Maharittha, the nephew of Devanampiya Tissa, announcing the message of the king as well as the *thera* to Dhammasoka thus spoke "Sovereign of elephants! the consort of the brother of thy ally, the king of Lanka impelled by the desire of devoting herself to the ministry of Buddha, is unremittingly leading the life of a pious devotee. For the purpose of ordaining her a priestess, deputing thither the *theri* Sanghamitta, send also with her the right branch of the great Bo-tree."

"The king thereupon thus meditated: It is not meet to lop with any weapon the great Bodhi-tree: by what means then can I obtain a branch thereof? This lord of the land, by the advice of the minister Mahadeva, having invited the priesthood to a repast, thus inquired of the high priest. "Lord, is it or is it not, meet to transmit a branch of the great bodhi tree to Lanka? The chief priest, the son of Moggali, replied, "It is fitting that it should be sent;" and expounded to the monarch the five important resolves of Buddha the deity gifted with five means of perception. The lord of the land, hearing this reply, rejoicing thereat, ordered the road to the Bo-tree, distant from Pataliputta seven yojanas, to be swept, and perfectly decorated in every respect; and for the purpose of having the vase made of collected gold, Vissakama himself, assuming character of a jewel and repairing thither inquired of what size shall the vase be constructed? On being told, make it, deciding on the size thyself," receiving the gold, he moulded it with his own hand, and instantly perfecting that vase, nine cubits in circumference five cubits in depth, three cubits in diameter, eight in thickness, and in the rim of the month of the thickness of the trunk of the full grown elephant, he departed.

The monarch causing that vase, resplendent like the meridian, sun, to be brought ; attended by the four constituent hosts of his military array, and by the great body of the priesthood, which extended over space of seven yojanas in length and three in breadth, repaired to the great Bo-tree; which was decorated with every variety of ornament; glittering with the variegated splendour of gems; decked with rows of streaming banners; laden with offerings of flowers of every hue; and surrounded by the sound of every description of music. Encircling it with this concourse of people, he screened the Bo-tree with a curtain. Surrounding himself and the great Bodhi-tree most completely with a body of a thousand priests who were the heads of fraternities, and with more than a thousand kings who had received anointment, he gazed on the great Bodhi-tree with clasped hands. Then the small branches of its right branch vanished, leaving only portions of about a cubit and the stem thereof adhering to the main trunk. Seeing this miracle the ruler of the world, overjoyed, exclaimed, "I make an offering of my empire to the great Bo-tree." The lord of the land thereupon invested the great Bo-tree with the empire. Making flower and other offerings to the great Bo-tree, he walked around it. Having bowed down with up-lifted hands at eight places, and placed that previous vase on a golden chair, studded with various gems, of such a height that the branch could be easily reached, he ascended it himself for the purpose of obtaining the supreme branch. Using vermilion in a golden pencil, and therewith making a streak on the branch, he made this solemn declaration and invocation: "If this supreme right Bo-branch from this Bo-tree is destined to depart from hence to the land of Lanka, and if my faith be unshaken in the religion of Buddha, then let it, self-severed instantly transplant itself into this golden vase."

The Bo-branch severing itself at the place where the streak was made, rested on the top of the vase (which was) filled with scented soil. The monarch then encircled the Branch with nine streaks above the original streak, at intervals of three inches; from the original streak the principal, and from the other streaks minor roots, ten from each, shooting forth like a net work, descended (into the soil in the vase). The sovereign, on witnessing this miracle, with uplifted hands set up a shout, while yet standing on the golden chair, which was echoed by the surrounding spectators. The delighted priesthood expressed their joy by shouts of sadhu, and the crowding multitude, waving thousands of cloth over their heads cheered.

The monarch, descending from the chair, and tarrying on the spot for seven days, unremitttingly kept up, in diverse ways, a festival of offering to the Bo-branch. This great monarch, overjoyed, a second time made an offerings of the empire to the great Bodhi.

On the fifteenth, being the full moon day of the bright half of the month Assayuja, the king took possession of the great Bo-branch. At the end of two weeks from that date the lord of chariots, having had his capital fully ornamented, and a superb hall built, placing the great Bo-branch in chariot, on that very day brought it in a procession of offerings. Thus did the great emperor of India, the Delight of the gods, 2200 years ago, show his veneration to the great Bodhi branch."

This sacred branch of the Bodhi Tree was taken by Sanghamitta to Sri Lanka, where it was ceremoniously planted by the king Devanampiya Tissa in the Mahamegha garden of his capital, Anuradhapura. Tended with honour and care through the ages, it flourishes to this day, and is one of the most sacred objects of veneration and worship for millions of Buddhists.

Devanampiya Tissa ruled for forty years, and Buddhism had taken deep roots in Sri Lanka during his eventful reign. In the subsequent centuries, Buddhism not only continued to flourish in the Island but it also gained vitality, and inspired some Sri Lankan monks to visit the Holy Seat of Buddha's Enlightenment in India. The first pilgrim from Sri Lanka, rather from any foreign country, to register his presence at Buddha Gaya was one Bodhirakshita who donated a crossbar to the railing, apparently to replace the one which had been broken. His brief inscription[1] on a rail-bar of the Old Stone-Railing reads as "The gift of Bodhirakshita of Sri Lanka."

As time rolled by, the flow of Buddhist pilgrims from Sri Lanka increased substantially but accommodation arrangements at Buddha Gaya being inadequate, these pilgrims were often put to inconvenience. In the fourth century AD, a brother of King Meghavana of Sri Lanka, who had become a monk, came on pilgrimage to Buddha Gaya, with a group of other pilgrims, and had to face a lot of difficulties at the Holy Seat of Buddha's Enlightenment. On return to Sri Lanka, he apprised the king of the lack of accommodation and other facilities for the Sri Lankan pilgrims at Buddha Gaya, and requested him to do something about it. Accordingly, the Sri Lankan King Meghavana (AD 362—389), sought permission from the Indian King, Samudragupta (AD 330—380), to build a rest house and monastery at Buddha Gaya for the use of the Sinhalese pilgrims. Permission having been granted by the Gupta King, the Sri

Lankan King built a magnificent monastery for the convenience of the pilgrims at Buddha Gaya, Hiuen Tsang, who saw this monastery in AD 637, says:

> "Outside the northern gate of the wall of the Bodhi Tree is the Mahabodhi *sangharama.* It was built by a former king of Sinhala (Ceylon). This edifice has six halls, with towers of observation (temple towers) of three storeys; it is surrounded by a wall of defence thirty or forty feet high. The utmost skill of the artist has been employed; the ornamentation is in the richest colours (red and blue). The statue of Buddha is cast of gold and silver, decorated with gems and precious stones. The stupas are high and large in proportion, and beautifully ornamented; they contain relics of Buddha." (Beal, Buddhist Records, 1981, II - ; 133.)

After the erection of the Sri Lankan Monastery (Mahabodhi sangharama) at Bodh Gaya, the flow of pilgrims from that Island country further increased but the inscriptional record that has survived on site tells us only of three important monk-pilgrims from Sri Lanka during the next three hundred years. Of these, the first pilgrim was Mahanama, the author of Mahavamsa, the celebrated chronicle of Sri Lanka composed in the fifth century AD. According to Cunningham, the historian Mahanama "was the uncle of Raja Dhatu Sena, the heir of Raja Mitra Sena, who was conquered and killed by the invader Pandu, in AD 433, when Dhatu Sena and his uncle escaped ... he may have visited the Bodhi Tree in Magadha, where he built a temple and dedicated a statue."

The inscription[2] of the first Mahanama begins with the usual formula in use during the Gupta period for the record of a religious gift:

> "This is the appropriate religious gift of the Sakya Bhikshu, the Sthavira Mahanaman, a resident of Amradvipa. Whatever religious merit may be in this (act), let it be for the acquisition of supreme knowledge by all sentient beings."

The second pilgrim was another Mahanama who came in the sixth century. The inscription left behind by him is rather longish, and bears the date, Samvat 269, that is, AD 587 (AD 318 + 269=587). This inscription[3], written in Sanskrit, can now be seen in the Indian Museum, Calcutta. It reads as :

> "Victorious for a very long time is that doctrine, replete with fame, of the Teacher, the chief kinsman of the Sakyas, by which lustrous as the full-moon, the inscrutable primary substance of

existence has been pervaded in all directions: by which the warriors, who are heretics, obstructive of the path of beautitude, have been broken to pieces, being assailed with the weapon logic; (and) by which the whole treasure of religion, that had been stolen by the enemy which is original in nature, has been recovered for the welfare of mankind!

(Line 2-3) — May he, Maha-Kasyapa, who is worthy of praise, protect you, — he who observed the precepts of (Buddha) the chief of saints; who practised that auspicious habits of abstract meditation which is of the nature of a trance; who overcame the anguish of successive states of existence; whose wonderful subjugation of the passions in final emancipation (is to be) displayed in the hand of Maitreya; and by whom the two pure feet of (Buddha) the saint were beheld at the time of attaining Nirvana!

(Line 4-5) — His disciples, endowed with a connected tradition of doctrine, purified as to (their) emotions, (and) active in compassion for existing beings, roamed at one time over the stainless country at the feet of the mountains of Lanka; and in succession from them there were born, in hundreds, disciples and disciples' disciples, possessed of the virtue of (good) character, who, without the glory of (actual) sovereignty, were the ornaments of a lofty race of kings.

(Line 6) — Then there was the Sramana Bhava, whose welfare was effected by the development of abstract meditation; who discriminated between good and evil, who destroyed error; (and) who possessed an unequalled wealth of true religion.

(Line 7-8) — And his disciple (was) he who had the name of Rahula; after whom (there came) the ascetic Upasena (I); then in succession (there was) Mahanaman (I) (and) after him another Upasena (II), whose special characteristic of affection, of the kind that is felt towards offspring, — for any distressed man who came to him for protection, and for any afflicted person whose fortitude had been destroyed by the continuous flight of the arrows of adversity — extended in conformity with the disposition of a kinsman, (even) to any cruel man who might seek to do (him) harm; (and) by whose fame, arising from good actions, the whole world was thus completely filled.

(Line 9, 10) — His disciple, greater (even than himself, (is) he who has the excellent name of Mahanaman (II); an inhabitant of

Amradvipa; a very ocean of a mighty family; born in the island of Lanka; delighting in the welfare of other; — by him this beautiful mansion of the teacher of mankind, who overcame the power of (the god) Samara, — dazzling white as the rays of the moon, with an open pavillion on all sides, — has been caused to be made at the exalted Bodhimanda.

(Line 11) — By means of this appropriate (action), let mankind, — freed from attachment to worldly things; having the condition of (mental) darkness dispelled; (and), like (the flame of) a torch, having no adhesion (to material objects), — enjoy the supreme happiness of perfect wisdom!

(Line 12-13) — As long as the sun, the dispeller of darkness, shines in all directions with diffused rays; as long as the ocean (is) full on all sides with its circles of waves that are curved like the hood of hooded snakes; and as long as (the mountain) Sumeru, the abode of (the god) Indra, has its summits made beautiful by various jewelled slabs, in such a way as to be full of lustre, — so long let this temple of the great saint attain the condition of being everlasting:

(Line 14) — The year 200 (and) 60 (and) 9; (the month) Caitra; the bright fortnight; the day seven."

Mahanama II had also built a small shrine with a Buddha statue, the remains of which can still be seen near the southern staircase leading to the Temple. The Buddha statue that Mahanama II had placed in the shrine has also been found.

The third important pilgrim from Sri Lanka was Prakhyatakirti, a distinguished monk, who came in the seventh century AD. He not only built a shrine but also repaired the Maha Bodhi Temple, and made provision to have a lamp burn perpetually within it. He also made gifts to the Sangha and performed a puja for peace in the world. His inscription[4] is in two parts, written on two separate stones of the railing.

The first part of the inscription reads as:

"The virtuous Sramana Prakhyatakirti having been a descendant of the rulers of the Island of Lanka (Sri Lanka) (has become) moon to the firmament of his family (v. 1).

This monk, through devotion, desirous of attaining Buddhahood, caused to be performed acts of worship at the Ratna-traya (the Buddhist Holy Triad) for the peace of mankind (v. 2).

Whatever merit has been acquired by me through this, let that be for the enlightenment of . . . Let that every auspicious reward be shared by (v. 3).

The second part of the inscriptions reads as:

(Line 1) — (A shrine) has been made (where the great Diamond-throne temple) is. The temple has been adorned with a new coating of plaster and paint at the cost of 250 dinars. And in the temple a lamp of ghee has been provided for the Lord Buddha by the gift of a hundred cows, for as long as the moon, sun and stars shall endure. Also by another hundred cows in addition to the cost of small, perpetually recurring repairs to the temple, provision has been made for another lamp of ghee, to be burnt daily before the image inside the temple. By another hundred cows provision has been made for having a lamp of ghee burnt before the brass image of the Lord Buddha in the monastery (vihara).

(Line 2.) — . . . a perpetual endowment of a lamp of ghee has been made for the benefit of the monastery. There also. a large water reservoir has been dug out for the use of the noble congregation of monks and to the east of it a new field has been laid out. Whatever merit may have been acquired by me by all this, may this be for the benefit of my parents at first . . . ."

When Hiuen Tsang visited Buddha Gaya in AD 637, he found more than 1000 monks residing in the Sri Lankan Monastery. About their conduct, he says, "They carefully observe the Dharma Vinaya, and their conduct was pure and correct." However, his statement that "they study the Great Vehicle and belong to the Sthavira (*Shang-tso-pu*) school" is not well-founded as Sri Lanka has all along been a citadel of the Theravada Buddhism, and was so at the time of Hiuen Tsang's visit.

The presence of a large number of Sri Lankan monks at Buddha Gaya proved a boon later as when Buddhism began to decline in India, they readily came forward to take care of the puja ceremonies at the sacred Maha Bodhi Temple. That the flag of Dhamma was kept aloft for a long time at Buddha Gaya by the Sri Lankan monks residing in the Sri Lankan Monastery is self-evident from two inscriptions of Indian kings. In the first inscription[5] dated in AD 1157, Asokaballa, the king of the Siwalik Hills in the Punjab, says:

"Moreover, for the offering to Buddha, the daily rations with pots, incense and lamps, shall be given so long as the Sun and Moon shall endure, by the leaders of the Ceylon Assembly in Mahabodhi. This offering must be prepared by the cook Mamaka, and the good keeper and disposer Harichandra."

The second inscription of an Indian king which tells us that the Great Maha Bodhi Temple was being looked after by a Sri Lankan monk, Mangalasvamin, is dated in the year 1202 AD. The donor says in the inscription[6]:

> "Hail! Majestic is the shade of the Bodhi Tree, ancient, bestower of great enlightenment to the Victors and which is the stay of those who are on the road to perfect enlightenment. This village of Katthala in Sataghatta, its lands, water, together with the plough tax is granted by charter to the Vajrasana for the monastery in trust to Venerable Mangalasvamin of Lanka, master of the Tipitaka, by the King, son of Buddhasena, for as long as the sun and moon endure."

The Sri Lankan Monastery continued to be in use till atleast the thirteenth century as Dharmasvamin, a Tibetan pilgrim, who visited Buddha Gaya in AD 1234 had stayed in this Monastery. It now lies under the large mound that extends from the Mahant's Math to the back of the Maha Bodhi Society Rest House and the Tibetan Temple. When excavated by Cunningham and Beglar in 1885, it was found to be a huge structure, 15 metres square with walls 3 metres thick, towers on the four corners and a pillard courtyard in the middle. A drain led from the courtyard to the outer walls and ended in a richly carved makkara, now in the Archaeological Museum. Surrounding the monastery and about 92 metres from it, was a huge wall with sixteen towers.

NOTES

1. Alexander Cunningham, Mahabodhi or the Great Buddhist Temple under the Bodhi Tree at Buddha Gaya, p. 16; Benimadhab Barua, Gaya and Buddha Gaya, vol. II, p. 68. The text and translation is :

Cunningham

Bodhi-rakhitasa Taba-pankasa danam

"Gift of Bodhi-rakshita of Tambaparna (Ceylon)."

B.M. Barua

Bodhirakhitasa Ta(ṃ)bapa(ṃ)nakasa dānam

"The gift of Bodhirakshita,— a man of Tampraparni (Ceylon or Tinnevelly region)."

2. Cunningham (Mahabodhi : 62) reads the inscription as follows :

Deya dharmmayaṁ Sākya-bhikshoh Âmra-dwipa-vāsi Sthâvira Mahanâmasya yadatra punyated bhavatu sarvvāsatmûnûm attarajna nivaptayestam.

"The religious gift of the Sakya mendicant, an inhabitant of Amradwipa, the Sthavira Mahanama. Whatever religious merit there may in this (act) let it be for the acquisition of supreme knowledge by all sentient beings."

Also see B.M. Barua, Gaya and Buddha Gaya, vol. II, p. 186.

3. The inscription of Mahanama II, in Sanskrit, as read and translated by J.F. Fleet (Corpus Inscriptionum Indicarum, Vol. III, p. 277) is as follows:

1. *Om (II) Vyāto yen* = ā-prameyaḥ sakala-śaśi-rucā sarvvataḥ sat(t)va- dhātuh kṣuṇṇāh pāṣaṇḍa-yodhas = sugati = patha = rudhas = tarkka = 'sastrā-bhiyuktaḥ sampūrṇṇo.
2. *dharmma-koṣaḥ prakṛti-ripu-hrtaḥ sādhito lokabhūtyai 1 śāstuḥ Śāky-aikava (ba)ndhor* = jjayati cirataraṁ tad = yaśas-sāra-tanttram 11 Nairod-hiṁ śubha-bhāvanā.
3. *m =anusṛtaḥ saṁsāra-sainkleśa-j in=Maitreyasya kare vimukti-vaśitā yasy =ādbutā vyākṛtā 1 nirvvāṇ-āvasare ca yena caraṇau ḍṛṣṭau muneḥ.*
4. *pāvanau 1 pāyād-vah sa maïndra-śāsana-dhara stutyo Mahā-Kāśyapah 11 Saṁyukt-āgamino visuddha-rajasaḥ sat (t) v-ānukamp-ōdyataḥ śiṣyā.*
5. *Yasya sakṛd = vicerur = amālaṁ Laācal-opatyakām tébhyaḥ śila-guṇ-ānvitāś = ca śaṭaśaḥ śiṣyā-preśiṣyāh kramāj = jātās-tunga-narendra-*
6. *Vaṁśa-tilakāh prostrjya rājya-śriyam 11 Dhyān-ōday-āhita-hitah śubh-āśubhavivekrd = vihȧta-mohaḥ sad-dharmm-ātula-vibhavo Bhavo va (ba) bhūva*
7. *śramaṇas-ṭataḥ 11 Rāhul-akhyāś-ca tac-chiṣya Upasonō yatir-yataḥ Mahānāma kramād-ēvam = Upssenas-tato-paraḥ 11 Vātsalyaṁ śaran-ā-*
8. *gatasya satataṁ dinasya vaiśe ṣikam vyāpat-sāyaka-santai-ksata-dhṛtēr =ārttasya c =āpatyakaṁ = kru-rasy = āhita-kāriṇaḥ pravitataṁ va (ba) dhōr = yathā-*
9. *bhāvatah evaṁ sac-carit-odbhavena yaśasa yasy =ācitaṁ bhūtalaṁ 11 Ämradvi -ādhivāsi pṛthu-kula-jaladhis = tasya śisyo mahiy ̄an.*
10. *Laṅka-dvipa-prasūtah parahita-nirataḥ san-Mahānama-nāmā 1 ten= ocair Vvo(bbo) dhimaṇde śaśi-kara-dhavalaḥ sarvvato maṇḍapena 1*
11. *Kāntaḥ prāsāda eṣa Smara-va(bh)-jayinaḥ kāritō loka-śastuḥ 1 Vyapagata-viṣaya-sneho hata-timira-daśaḥ pradipa-vad-a-saṅgaḥ*
12. *kuśalēn =ānena jano vo(bo) dhi-sukham-anuttaraṁ bhajatām 11 Yāvad-dhvānt-āpahāri pravitata-kiraṇaḥ sarvvato bhāti bhāsvān = yavat = pūṃṇō = mvu (mbu)*
13. *rāśiḥ phaṇi-phaṇa-kuṭilair=ūrmmi-cakkrais=samantāt yāvac = c = Endrādhivāso vividha-maṇi-śilā cāru-srngan Sumeraḥ śōbh-āḍhyam.*
14. *tāvad = ētad = bhavanam = uru-muneḥ śāsvaṭvam = prayātu 11 Samvat 200 60 9 Caitra śu di 7 11*

(Please also see Cunningham, Mahabodhi: 60-61)

4. The first part of the inscription of Prakhyatakirtti on the Coping of the Old Stone-Railing, as read by Bloch is as follows:

(Line-1) — *Laṅkādvipa-narendrānāṃ śramanaḥ kulajo'- bhavat* (*l*)

Prakhyatakirttir-ddharmātmāsvakulāmbara-candramāh (II)

Bhaktyā tu bhukṣuṇā-nena buddhatvam - abhikāṃkṣatā (I)

kārā ratnatraye samyak-kār iā śāntaye nṛṇām (II)

Tato mayā yat-kuśalaṃ hyupārjjitaṃ

tad astyupādh(ya) ya v-v-v-v-v-

v-v--vv-v-

(Line 2) *Śubhena tenaiva (pha)lena yujyatām* (II)

The second part of the same inscription as read by Bloch is as follows:

(Line 1) — . . .*kārito yatra Vajrāsana-vṛhad-gandhakuṭi(.) Prāsadamarddha-trikair-dināraśaṭais-sudhā-lepya- punar-ṇavīkaraṇena saṃskṛtaṃ(.) Atraiva ca pratyahaṃ ācandrārkkatārakaṃ Bhagavato Buddhāya go-śata- dānena ghṛta-pradīpaḥ ākāritaḥ(.) Prāṣāde khaṇḍa-sphaṭita pratisamārādhana tat-pratimāyāṁ ca pratyahaṁ ghṛta*
-pradipo go-śatenā-parena ākāritah(.) Vihārepi Bhagavato raitya-Buddha-pratimāyaṃ go-śatenạ ghṛta-pradipaḥ. . .(.)

(Line 2.) —. . . *(ghṛta)-pradipākasayanīvi-nibandhaḥ vihāro-payogāya kārita-Tatra-pi. . .bhikusaṃ ghasya (ārya)-sya ((u) payogya mahāntam-ādhāram khanitaṃ* (.)

tadanupūrṇaṃ caprahataka-ksetram-utpāditaṃ (.)

Tad-et at sarvvaṃ yan-ṃayā punyopacita-sambhāraṃ kśtvā. . .(.)

(Bloch, ASR., 1908-9: 153; Cunningham, Mahabodhi, 1892: 23; B.M. Barua, Gaya and Buddha Gaya, 1934: 71-72)

The second part of this inscription was earlier considered by the scholars as an independent Mediaeval Inscription. However, now this undated and unnamed inscription is recognised as second part of Prakhyatakirti's inscription. (Cf. S. Dhammika, Middle Land Middle Way, 1992: 55)

5. Cunningham, Mahabodhi; 1892, reprint 1972: 79.

6. S. Dhammika, Middle Land Middle Way, 1992: 58. This inscription was discovered at Janibigha in Bihar, Cf. Journal of the Bihar and Orissa Research Society, vol. iv, p. 279; D.K. Barua, Buddha Gaya Temple—Its History, 1975 p. 24.

Chapter V

CHINESE PILGRIMS IN BUDDHA GAYA

(i) Fa-hian

Fa-hian (also written as Fa-hien or Fa-hsein), the first Chinese pilgrim, who came to India in search of real Buddhism had left China in AD 399. He practically walked all the way from Central China across the Gobi desert, over the Hindu Kush, and entered India via Afghanistan in 406. Before he went back in 411, Fa-hian had almost visited all the important Buddhist sites and shrines in India. His tour-notes have come to us in "The Travels of Fa-hsien or Record of the Buddhist Kingdoms," translated from the Chinese by H.A. Giles. This is what Fa-hian writes (Giles, reprint 1972: 54-56) about the Buddha Gaya shrine which he visited in 409 AD:

"Half a yojana to the north-east of this, the pilgrims arrived at the cave in which Buddha as a Bodhisattva sat down cross-legged with his face to the west, and reflected as follows: "If I am to become a Buddha, there should be some divine manifestation in token thereof." At once the silhouette of a Buddha appeared upon the rock; it was over three feet in height and is plainly visible at the present day. Then heaven and earth quaked mightily, and the devas in the empyrean made the following announcement: "This is not the place where past and future Buddhas have attained or are to attain Buddhaship. The proper spot is less than half a yojana to the south-west of this, beneath the Bo (palm) tree, where all past and future Buddhas have attained or will attain to Buddhaship." When the devas had uttered these words, they proceeded to lead the way with singing, in order to conduct the Bodhisattva thither. He then got up and followed; and when thirty paces from the tree, a deva gave him the grass of happy omen (*kusa*). Having accepted this, he went on fifteen paces further, and then five hundred green birds came and flew three times round him, and departed. The Bodhisattva went on to the Bo tree; and there, laying down the grass of happy omen, he took his seat with his face to the east. Then Mara, king of the devils, sent three beautiful girls, who approached him from the north to tempt him, while Mara himself came from the south for the same purpose. But the Bodhisattva pressed the ground with his toes, whereupon the infernal army retreated in confusion, and the three girls were changed into old women.

At the above-mentioned place where Buddha suffered self-mortification for six years, as well as at these other spots, men of later ages have raised pagodas and set up images, all of which are still in existence. Pagodas have also been raised at the following places: where Buddha, then a Bodhisattva, after having attained Buddhaship, contemplated the Bo tree for seven days, experiencing the joy of liberation from earthly trammels; where Buddha paced east and west beneath the Bo tree for seven days; where the devas caused to appear a chamber built from the seven preciosities and there made offerings to Buddha for seven days; where the blind dragon, Muchilinda, coiled round Buddha for seven days to shelter him; where Buddha sat facing the east on a square rock under a fig-tree when Brahma came and begged him to expound the Faith; where the four heavenly kings offered to Buddha their alms-bowls; where the five hundred traders gave him boiled grain and honey; and where he converted the brothers Kasyapa with their disciples to the number of one thousand souls.

Where Buddha attained to Buddhaship, there are three monasteries, each with resident priests, who receive offerings in abundance from the populace, without the least stint. The strictness with which, while Buddha was still in the world, the holy brotherhood observed their vows and disciplinary regulations, and the gravity of their deportment when sitting, rising, or entering an assembly, persist down to the present day.

Ever since Buddha entered into Nirvana, the sites of four great pagodas have been handed down by unbroken tradition; namely (1) On the spot where Buddha was born, (2) where he became a Lo-han, (3) where he preached the Faith, and (4) where he passed away."

(ii) Hiuen Tsang

Hiuen Tsang (also written as Hiuen Tsiang, Hsuan-tsang, Yuan Chwang, or Xuanzang), the celebrated second Chinese pilgrim, who came to India after about 230 years of Fa-hian, was a very keen observer and has left for us the most valuable record of India in general, and Buddhism in particular, the religion which he loved. Hiuen Tsang left China in AD 629, at the age of 26, and took the same route to India ss Fa-hian had done, across the Central Asia, the Gobi desert and the Hindu Kush mountains. As he had been refused permission by the Chinese Emperor to leave China, he travelled secretly within China, hiding by day and travelling by night. When he crossed over to Turfan, the first kingdom in Central Asia, Hiuen Tsang was welcomed by the king, who was a devout Buddhist. The Turfan king, after vainly trying to keep Hiuen Tsang in his kingdom, provided him with an escort for his further journey. Thus assured of protection, Hiuen Tsang marched forward, and after crossing the Hindu Kush, reached Bamiyan in Afghanistan. From Bamiyan, Hiuen Tsang came, after the summer of AD 630 to Nagarhara, modern Jalalabad, in Afghanistan. From here, he begins his account of India. Hiuen Tsang was in India for the next 14 years, and during that period, he travelled all over India, visiting almost all the Buddhist monasteries, viharas etc. and keeping notes of what he saw at each and every place. His detailed account of almost all the Buddhist sites and shrines in India at the time of his visit has come to us in "*SI-YU-KI*-Buddhist Records of the Western World" Translated from the Chinese of Hiuen Tsang by Samuel Beal, in two volumes. Here is the description of what he saw at Buddha Gaya in AD 637:

"Going south-west from Mount Pragbodhi about 14 or 15 li, we come to the Bodhi Tree. It is surrounded by a brick wall (a wall of piled bricks) of considerable height, steep and strong. It is long from east to west, and short from north to south. It is about 500 paces round. Rare trees with their renowned flowers connect their shade and cast their shadows; the delicate sha herb and different shrubs carpet the soil. The principal gate opens to the east, opposite the Nairanjana river. The southern gate adjoins a great flowery bank. The western side is blocked up and difficult of access (steep and strong). The northern gate opens into the great Sangharama. Within the surrounding wall the sacred traces touch one another in all directions. Here there are Stupas, in another place Viharas. The kings, princes, and great personages throughout all Jambudvipa, who have accepted the bequeathed teaching as handed down to them, have erected these monuments as memorials.

In the middle of the enclosure surrounding the Bodhi Tree is the diamond throne (Vajrasana). In former days, when the Bhadra-kalpa was arriving at the period of perfection (*vivartta*), when the great earth arose, this (throne) also appeared. It is in the middle of the great chiliocosm; it goes down to the limits of the golden wheel (the gold circle), and upwards it is flush with the ground. It is composed of diamond. In circuit it is 100 paces or so. On this the thousand Buddhas of the Bhadra-kalpa have sat and entered the diamond Samadhi; hence the name of the diamond throne. It is the place where the Buddhas attain the holy path (the sacred way of Buddhahood). It is also called the Bodhimanda. When the great earth is shaken, this place alone is unmoved. Therefore when Tathagata was about to reach the condition of enlightenment, and he went successively to the four angles of this enclosure, the earth shook and quaked; but afterwards coming in this spot, all was still and at rest. From the time of entering on the concluding portion of the Kalpa, when the true law dies out and disappears, the earth and dust begin to cover over this spot, and it will be no longer visible.

The Bodhi Tree above the diamond throne is the same as the Pippala tree. In old days, when Buddha was alive, it was several hundred feet in height. Although it has often been injured by cutting, it still is 40 or 50 feet in height. Buddha sitting under this tree reached perfect wisdom, and therefore it is called the (*Samyak sambodhi*) tree of knowledge (*Pu-ti-Bodhi*). The bark is of a yellowish-white colour; the leaves, and twigs of a dark green. The leaves wither not either in winter or summer, but they remain shining and glistening all the year round without change. But at every successive Nirvana-days (of the Buddha) the leaves wither and fall, and then in a moment revive as before. On this day (of the Nirvana) the princes of different countries and the religious multitude from different quarters assemble by thousands and ten thousands unbidden, and bathe (the roots) with scented water and perfumed milk; whilst they raise the sounds of music and scatter flowers and perfumes, and whilst the light of the day is continued by the burning torches, they offer their religious gifts.

To the east of the Bodhi Tree there is a vihara about 160 or 170 feet high. Its lower foundation-wall is 20 or more paces in its face. The building (pile) is of blue tiles (bricks) covered with chunam (burnt stone lime): all the niches in the different storeys hold golden figures. The four sides of the building are covered with wonderful ornamental work; in one place figures of stringed pearls (garlands), in another figures of heavenly Rishis. The whole is surrounded by a gilded copper *Amalaka* fruit. The easter face adjoins a storeyed pavillion, the projecting eaves of which rise one over the other to the height of three distinct chambers; its projecting eaves, its pillars, beams, doors, and windows are decorated with gold and silver ornamental work, with pearls and gems let in to fill up interstices. Its sombre chambers and mysterious halls have doors in each of the three storeys. To the right and left of the outside gate are niches like chambers; in the left is a figure of Avalokitesvara Bodhisattva, and in the right a figure of Maitreya (*T'se-shi*) Bodhisattva. They are made of white silver, and are about 10 feet high. On the site of the present vihara Asoka-raja at first built a small vihara.

Sasanka-raja having cut down the Bodhi Tree, wished to destroy the image; but having seen its loving features, his mind had no rest or determination, and he returned with his retinue homewards.

The figure still exists in its perfect state as it was made by the sacred art of the god. It stands in a dark chamber; lamps and torches are kept burning therein; but those who wish to see the sacred features cannot do so by coming into the chamber; they should in the morning reflect the sunlight by means of a great mirror of the interior of the room; the sacred marks may then be seen. Those who behold them find their religious emotions much increased.

To the north of the Bodhi Tree is a spot where Buddha walked up and down. When Tathagata had obtained enlightenment, he did not rise from the throne, but remained perfectly quiet for seven days, lost in contemplation. Then rising, he walked up and down during seven days to the north of the tree; he walked there east and west for a distance of ten paces or so. Miraculous flowers sprang up under his foot-traces to the number of eighteen. Afterwards this space was covered in by a brick wall about three feet high.

On the left side of the road, to the north of the place where Buddha walked, is a large stone, on the top of which, as it stands in a great vihara, is a figure of Buddha with his eyes raised and looking up. Here in former times Buddha sat for seven days contemplating the Bodhi Tree he did not remove his gaze from it during this period, desiring thereby to indicate his grateful feelings towards the tree by so looking at it with fixed eyes.

Not far to the west of the Bodhi Tree is a large vihara in which is a figure of Buddha made of teou-shih (brass), ornamented with rare jewels; he stands with his face to the east. Before it is a blue stone with wonderful marks upon it and strangely figured. This is (the place where) Buddha sat on a seven-gemmed throne made by Sakra Deva-raja when Brahmaraja built a hall for him of seven precious substances, after he had arrived at complete enlightenment. Whilst he thus sat for seven days in reflection the mysterious glory which shone from his person lit up the Bodhi tree. From the time of the holy one till the present is so long that the gems have changed into stone.

Not far to the south of the Bodhi tree is a stupa about 100 feet high, which was built by Asoka-raja. Budhisattva having bathed in the Nairanjana river, proceeded towards the Bodhi tree. Then he thought, "What shall I do for a seat? I will seek for some pure rushes when the day breaks". Then Sakaraja transformed himself into a grass-cutter, who, with his burden on his back went along the road. Bodhisattva addressing him said, "Can you give me the bundle of grass you are carrying on your back?"

The assumed grass-cutter, hearing the request, offered the grass with respect, Bodhisattva having received it, went onwards to the tree.

No far to the north of this spot is a stupa. Bodhisattva, when about to obtain enlightenment (the fruit of Buddha), saw a flock of the blue birds rising up (rohin?) according to the lucky way. Of all the good omens recognised in India this is the most so. Therefore the Devas of the pure abodes (Suddhavasa) accommodated their proceedings to the customary modes of the world, and caused the birds thus to encircle him as spiritually (miraculously) indicating his holiness.

To the east of the Bodhi Tree, on the left and right of the great road, there are two stupas (one on each side). This is the place where Mara-raja tempted Bodhisattva. Bodhisattva, when on the point of enlightenment, was tempted by Mara to become a Chakravarttin (*Lun-wang*) monarch. On his refusing, he went away heavy and sorrowful. On this, his daughters, asking him, went to try to entice the Bodhisattva, but by his spiritual power he changed their youthful appearance into that of decrepit old women. Then leaning together on their sticks they went away.

To the north-west of the Bodhi tree in a vihara is the image of Kasyapa Buddha. It is noted for its miraculous and sacred qualities. From time to time it emits a glorious light. The old records say, that if a man actuated by sincere faith walks round it seven times he obtains the power of knowing the place and condition of his (former?) births.

To the north-west of the wall of the Bodhi Tree is a stupa about 40 feet high; it was built by a merchant chief (*Sreshthi*) of the country of *Tsao-kiu-Ch'u* (Tsaukuta).

At the south-east angle of the wall of the Bodhi Tree is a stupa by the side of Nyagrodha (*ni-ken-liu*) tree. Beside it, there is a vihara in which is a sitting figure of Buddha. This is the spot where the great Brahmadeva exhorted Buddha, when he had first acquired enlightenment, to turn the wheel of the excellent law.

At the south-west of the Bodhi Tree, outside the walls, there is a stupa; this is where the old house of the two shepherd-girls stood who offered the rice-milk to Buddha. By the side of it is another stupa where the girls boiled the rice; by the side of the stupa Tathagata received the rice. Outside the south gate of the Bodhi Tree is a great tank about 700 paces round, the water of which is clear and pure as a mirror.

Still to the south there is a tank; formerly, when Tathagata had just acquired perfect enlightenment, he wished to bathe; then Sakra (*shi*), king of Deva, for Buddha's sake, caused a pond to appear as a phantom.

On the west is a great stone where Buddha washed his robes, and then wished to dry them; on this, Sakra, king of Devas, brought this rock from the great Snowy Mountains. By the side of this is a stupa; this is where Tathagata put on (?) the old garments offered to him. Still to the south in a wood is a stupa; this is where the poor old woman gave the old garments which Tathagata accepted.

To the east of the pond which Sakra caused to appear, in the midst of a wood, is the lake of the Naga king Muchilinda (*Mu-chi,-lin-t'o*). The water of this lake is of a dark blue colour, its taste is sweet and pleasant; on the west bank is a small vihara in which is a figure of Buddha. Formerly, when Tathagata first acquired complete enlightenment, he sat on this spot in perfect composure, and for seven days dwelt in ecstatic contemplation. Then this Muchilinda Naga-raja kept guard over Tathagata; with his folds seven times round the body of Buddha, he caused many heads to appear, which over-shadowed him as a parasol; therefore to the east of this lake is the dwelling of the Naga.

To the east of the tank of Muchilinda in a vihara standing in a wood is a figure of Buddha, which represents him as thin and withered away.

At the side of this is the place where Buddha walked up and down, about 70 paces or so long, and on each side of it is a Pippala tree.

By the side of the Pippala tree which denoted the place of Buddha's fast is a stupa; this is where Ajnata-Kaundinya and the rest, to the number of five resided. When first the prince left his home, he wandered through the mountains and plains; he rested in forests and by wells of water. Then

Suddhodana-raja ordered five men to follow him and wait on his person. The prince having entered on his penance, then Ajnata Kaundinya and the rest gave themselves also to a diligent practice of the same.

To the south-west of this spot there is a stupa. This is where Bodhisattva entered the Nairanjana river to bathe. By the side of the river, not far off, is the place where Bodhisattva received the rice-milk.

By the side of this is a stupa where the merchant-prince (householder) offered him the wheat and honey.

By the side of the merchant-offering place is a stupa. This is the spot where the four Deva-rajas presented (Buddha) with a patra.

Not far from this spot is a stupa. This is the place where Tathagata preached the law for the sake of his mother. When Tathagata had acquired complete enlightenment, he was termed "The teacher of gods and of men." His mother, Maya, then came down from heaven to this place. The Lord of the World preached to her according to the occasion, for her profit and pleasure.

Beside this spot is a dry pool, on the border of which is a stupa. This is where in former days Tathagata displayed various spiritual changes to convert those who were capable of it.

By the side of this spot is a stupa. Here Tathagata converted Uruvilva-Kasyapa (Yeu-leu-pin-li-kia-she-po) with his two brothers and a thousand of their followers.

To the north-west of the spot where the Kasyapa brothers were converted is a stupa. This is the place where Tathagata overcame the fiery Naga to which Kasyapa sacrified.

To the south of the tank of Muchilinda Naga is a stupa. This indicates the spot where Kasyapa went to save Buddha during an inundation.

Embarking in a boat to go to his deliverance, he saw the Lord of the World walking on the water as on land; and as he advanced down the stream, the waters divided and left the ground visible. Kasyapa having seen the miracle, his heart was subdued, and he returned.

By the side of the eastern gate of the wall of the Bodhi Tree is a stupa. This is where Mara-raja tried to frighten Bodhisattva. When first Mara-raja knew that Bodhisattva was about to obtain perfect enlightenment, having failed to confuse him by enticements or so terrify him by his arts, he summoned his host of spirits and arranged his demon army, and arrayed his soldiers, armed their weapons, as if to destroy the Bodhisattva. On this the winds arose and the rains descended, the thunders rolled in space and the lighting gleamed, as it lit up the darkness: flames of fire and clouds of smoke burst forth; sand and hailstones fell like lances, and were as arrows flying from the bow. Whereupon the Bodhisattva entered the samadhi of "great love," and changed the weapons of the host to lotus flowers. Mara's army, smitten by fear, retreated fast and disappeared.

Not far from this are two stupas build by Sakra, king of Devas, and by Brahma-raja.

Outside the northern gate of the wall of the Bodhi Tree is the Mahabodhi Sangharama. It was built by a former king of Sinhala (Ceylon). The edifice has six halls, with towers of observation (temple towers) of three storeys; it is surrounded by a wall of defence thirty or forty feet high. The utmost skill of the artist has been employed; the ornamentation is in the richest colours (red and blue). The statue of Buddha is cast of gold and silver, decorated with gems and precious stones. The stupas are high and large in proportion, and beautifully ornamented; they contain relics of Buddha. The bone relics are as great as the fingers of the hand, shining and smooth, of a pure white colour and translucent. The flesh relics are like the great true pearl, of a bluish-red tint. Every year on the day of the full moon of (the month when) Tathagata displayed great spiritual changes, they take these relics out for public exhibition. On these occasions sometimes a bright light is diffused, sometimes, it rains flowers. The priests of this convent are more than 1000 men; they study the great Vehicle and belong to the Sthavira (*Shang-tso-pu*) school. They carefully observe the Dharma Vinaya, and their conduct is pure and correct.

Every year when the Bhikshus break up their yearly rest of the rains, religious persons come here from every quarter in thousands and myriads, and during seven days and nights they scatter flowers, burn incense, and sound music as they wander through the district and pay their worship and present their offerings."

(Beal, Buddhist Records, reprint 1981, Vol. II, pp. 115-136).

Hiuen Tsang went back in 644 by crossing Punjab by way of Jalandhar and Taxila taking the same route across the Hindu Kush through the Central Asian States. He reached China in the spring of 645 and was received with great honour by the people of his country. Hiuen

Tsang took back with him a large number of Buddhist works, primarily in Sanskrit, carried by twenty-two horses. He spent the rest of his life in a monastery, specially built for him and his fellow translators in the then capital of China. While staying in that monastery, Hiuen Tsang exchanged letters with the chief monk of the Mahabodhi monastery at Bodh Gaya in the year AD 652-654. Initiative in this regard was taken by Prajna-deva, the head of the Maha Bodhi monastery, who wrote first and sent the letter through a messenger going to China. This letter reached Hiuen Tsang in 652. In this letter, Prajna-deva, who had not only met Hiuen Tsang during his sojourn in India but had also clashed with him at a great debate held in the royal court of Harsha, addressed Hiuen Tsang in these words:

"Maha-sthavira (the senior and distinguished monk) Prajna-deva who is surrounded by the well-known in the Maha-bodhi monastery at the Vajrasana (adamant seat, spot where Gautama became the Buddha, the enlightened one) of the subtle and auspicious World-honoured One sends his greetings to the Moksh-acharya of Mahachina who has achieved a subtle understanding of the boundless Tripitaka, and wishes Your Reverend good health and happiness.

I, Bhikshu Prajna-deva, have composed a hymn in praise of the great divine power of the Buddha, as well as the sutras and sastras, and the comparative merit of Buddha-dharma. I have entrusted Bhikshu Dharma-dirgha(?) (*Fa-ch'ang*) to bring the hymn to you.

The profoundly learned Acharya Janana-prabha here also sends his regards, and Upaska Surya-labdha also salutes you. We jointly send you two rolls of white cotton cloth to show our affection. As the distance is great, we pray that you will accept them without minding the meagreness.

If you require any scriptures, kindly send a list, and we shall make copies and send them to you.

Regards to Moksh-acharya."

Hiuen Tsang responded to this letter by way of his letter dated the 2nd month, AD 654. In his letter, Hiuen Tsang throws valuable light as to how he and Ven. Prajna-deva had participated in a debate in the court of Harsha and forcefully expressed each other's view point. He wrote:

"Bhikshu Hiuen-tsang of the great T'ang Empire begs to address this to the venerable Tripitaka-Master Prajna-deva of the Maha-bodhi monastery.

Your Reverend, it has been quite long since we parted, which enhances my longing and admiration for you. The non-communication between us all the more leaves the thirst of the yearning unquenched.

Bhikshu Dharma-dirgha arrived here with your very kind letter which brought me delight. There were also two rolls of fine cotton cloth and one fascimile of a hymn. I feel rather embarrassed as my want of virtue does not deserve such kindness.

The weather is getting warmer now, and I didn't know how you have been keeping since you last wrote.

I can imagine how you have assimilated the theories of all the schools, pondered over all volumes of the scriptures, hoisted the flag of the right dharma, led the swerving people to the correct path, and beat back the discordant preachers. You surely maintain your spirit in front of princes and nobles, and compliment or criticize at will in a galaxy of talented people. All this contributes to your highly pleasant demeanour.

As for me, incapacity is compounded by the decline of vigour. This all the more increases my yearnings when I remember the virtue of Your Reverend.

During my sojourn in your country, I had the honour of meeting Your Reverend. In the convocation of Kanya-kubja, we also engaged in a debate and argued out our respective view-points in the presence of the princes and thousands of devotees. As one of us expounded the tenets of the Mahayana School, the other advocated the aims of Hinayana. In the course of debate, our arguments unavoidably got heated. In order to defend the truth, there was scant regard for personal feelings. Thus, there were clashes. But, as soon as the debate was over, we did not take each other amiss. Now, you have sent word through the messenger apologizing for the past. How scrupulous you are!

You, holy sir, are profound in scholarship, eloquent in speech, firm in belief, and superb in cultivation. You are (in excellence) greater than the expanse of the water in the Anavatapa lake, and purer than the purest mani (jewel). Your Reverend set an example for emulation by the juniors among whom Your Reverend stood like a giant.

I wish you all the best in your endeavour in promoting the noble tradition and disseminating the true dharma.

Now, there is a messenger returning to India, I send you my sincere regards and a little momento as a token of my gratitude. It is too inadequate to express my deep feelings for Your Reverend. I hope Your Reverend would appreciate this.

When I was returning from India, I lost a horse-load of scriptures in the river Sindhu. I attach herewith a list and request that they be sent to me. This much for the present."[1]

(iii) Yuan-chan and Hwui Lun

While Hiuen Tsang was still in India, another Chinese pilgrim *Yuan-Chan* entered India in AD 638 from the north-west, via Jalandhar, and after spending four years at Mahabodhi returned to China. In AD 665 he came back to India, and once more visited Mahabodhi and the Vajrasana throne.

Another Chinese pilgrim *Hwui Lun* followed *Yuan-chan* and visited the Maha Bodhi Temple and the Vajrasana throne in AD 640.

(iv) I-tsing

I-tsing, the third well-known Chinese pilgrim, was about ten years of age when Hiuen Tsang returned to China. He became a Buddhist monk at the age of fourteen, and left China for India in AD 671 when he was in his thirty-seventh year. *I-tsing* took sea route to India, and after spending some time on the way in Sumatra, Srivijaya and Malaya, he landed at Tamralipti in 673, and thence went to Magadha and worshipped at Buddha Gaya and other sacred places. He spent ten years at Nalanda, and left India in AD 685 again taking the sea route by way of Tamralipti. About his visit to the Maha Bodhi Temple, *I-tsing* writes:

> "Afterwards we came to the Mahabodhi Vihara, near the Bodhi Tree, and worshipped the image of the real face (of the Buddha). I took stuffs of thick and fine silk, which were presented by the monks and laymen of Shah-tung, made a *kashaya* (yellow robe) of them of the size of the Tathagata and myself offered this robe to the Image. Many myriads of (small) canopies (also), which were entrusted to me by the Vinaya-master Hiuen of Pu, I presented on his behalf. The Dhyana-master An-Tao of Ts'ao charged me to worship the image of Bodhi, and I discharge the duty in his name. Then I prostrated myself entirely on the ground with an undivided mind, sincere and respectful. First I wished for China that the four kinds of benefits should widely prevail among all sentient beings in

1 (The letters of Prajnadeva and Hiuen Tsang were first of all translated from the Chinese into English by Professor Tan Chung and published by the China Academy, 1923, reprint Taipei, 1963. These letters have been reproduced in full by D. Devahuti in Harsha–A Political Study, Oxford University Press, Delhi, pp. 281-285.)

the region of the Law (*Dharmadhatu*), and I expressed my desire for a general reunion under the Naga-tree to meet the honoured (Buddha) Maitreya and to conform to the true doctrine, and then to obtain the knowledge that is not subject to births. I went round to worship all the holy places.''

(Tarakushu, J, 1966 ; pp. xxxii-xxxiii).

(v) Chi I

After a lapse of nearly four centuries, it was in the eleventh century that Buddha Gaya witnessed a great onrush of the Chinese pilgrims. At least five Chinese pilgrims have left their records by way of inscriptions in the Chinese language. The first to come in this wave was *Chi I,* a monk of the Great Han country. He came in about AD 1000 during the reign of the Mahipala I (AD 980-1020) of the Pala dynasty. In his inscription, *Chi I* says that

> ''Having first vowed to exhort or encourage 30,000 men to prepare themselves by their conduct for a birth in the heaven, to distribute in charity 30,000 books relating to a heavenly birth, himself to recite as many books, then in company with others, travelled through India, arrived in Magadha, where he gazed upon the diamond throne and other sacred vestiges of his religion. After this, in company with some other monks, he further vowed to continue his travels through India, for the same purpose.''

This inscription, consisting of three lines of Chinese characters, was found carved on a block of stone below a row of seven standing Buddhas and the Bodhisattva Maitreya. Two companions of *Chi-I* were named *Kwei-tseih,* and *Kwang-fung.*

(vi) Yun-shu

In 1021, a large party of the Chinese pilgrims led by *Che-yi,* who had taken a vow to do such meritorious deeds, as would lead to their birth in the Tushita heaven, arrived in Buddha Gaya. One of them, *Yun-shu,* a monk from the Western River i.e., Yellow River, of the Great Sung Empire in China, reciter of the Sutras, composed a long devotional hymn in praise of the Buddha and the Diamond Throne, and had it inscribed on a large stone tablet. *Yun-shu* says in the inscription:

''I *Yun shu,* having come from my far distance fatherland[1]. to gaze upon the territory of ''Buddha; and then having seen with my eyes the

1 That is, having accomplished the long and dangerous journey from China to India overland ?

miraculous footprint, was I not respectfully to offer my homage in glorification of my Teacher? I therefore collected together what of money I could spare, and some 30 paces to the north of the Bodhidruma[1] I raised a stone to the Ten Thousand Buddhas.

On the three occasions *Chiang Hsia-pias* spent here the season of fast; but he had not the wherewithal to express his deepfelt gratitude and overflowing respect, and was forced to content himself with eulogistic utterance upon the countenance of the birthless intelligence. He said:

O great Master, Merciful to the people, sympathising with all creatures.

Although thou dost not manifest thyself, still thou art a most efficacious God.

The herd of evil ones gaze up towards thee and recognize thy universal love.

Increasing with the changing moons of the past two thousand years."

He also said:

Oh, I could gaze on thy *lakshana* [2] for ever.

The majesty of thy countenance is rare indeed;

The crown of thy head is of fine serpentine;

Thy eyes like lotus flowers in a pool;

The *Swastika* [3] is written in gold upon thy breast;

The down on thy shoulders is like threads of snow;

Wonderful indeed is thy marvellous hand;

The texture of thy robes is impermeable to dust and smoke.

And as Chiang Hsia-pias had hymned the shadow, I determined to pronounce an eulogium on the body, of which Buddha has three in all. And I began with the *Nirvana-kaya* [4] as follows:

Deep is thy sympathy, genuine as the face of the moon;

Thou hast saved mortals from out of the midst of fire;

---

1 The famous Bodhi Tree, near Gaya, under which Shakyamuni Buddha obtained bodhi or enlightenment.
2 Thirty two characteristic marks which are found upon the body of every Buddha.
3 The mystic symbol?
4 That body which has the power of assuming any shape of man or animal & c.

Thou handest down the traditions of the healing art:

Thou stringest pearls in branching relationships.

The Three Vehicles lead the way to wisdom.

The five precepts brush away thy confusing dust of the world:

Mental disturbance extinguishes the light of the intellect.

But reaches not thy body, which is beyond the pale of matter.

I then proceeded to hymn the *Samboga-kaya,* [1] as follows:

The myriad priests in the garden of *Jeta.* [2]

Released from mortality, pass from the thraldom of desire.

The dust of this earth is wiped away:

They long to enter into possession of the middle kingdom.

The body of every Buddha possesses illimitable potentialities:

His heart is dissevered from all ties:

Cast for ever into the sea of the *Trilokaya* [3]

Personal ambitions are entirely obliterated.

I finally went on to eulogise the *Dharma-kaya* [4] as follows:

To witness the source and wander over the sphere of the Law

It was well to travel through dust and desert,

Bright, bright, without beginning or end;

Dark, dark, breaking the chain of *nidana*; [5]

Dwelling on earth without becoming earthy:

Abiding in heaven without undergoing change;

In this eulogium I utter the deepest words of my heart,

For I have at length met with the Immaculate Body.

And when I had eulogised the Triple Body, I desired also to eulogise the throne of each body, wherefore I proceeded to eulogise the shrine of *Nirmana-kaya* as follows:

There are wondrous foot prints in the Five Heavens,

---

1 That body which represents the merit and consequent reward of every Buddha.
2 Near Sravasti: a favourite resort of Buddha, Jetavana.
3 The regions of lust, form, and formlessness.
4 The spiritual body of every Buddha.
5 The everlasting chain of cause and effect.

Produced within the limits of the six cardinal points,
In depth descending to the bottom of the golden *chakkra,*[1]
In height reaching to the surface of the earth;
Never do any mortal cares mingle there,
For how can fire and water blend?
Sometimes the armies of Maitreya and Mara fight,
Until the latter are quelled by the roar of the lion.
I then eulogised the shrine of *Sambhoga-kaya* as follows:
This shrine towers above the limits of the *Trilo-kaya;*
Its shapely summit rests above the sky,
The *Kalpa*[2] of fire exercises no influence over it;
On earth how should we seek to model its like?
The reputation of king Asoka extends afar;
He rested in wonderful perception of the doctrine
A jewel among grains of sand,
Immortal, he will permeate the Great Void.

I then eulogised the shrine of the *Dharma-kaya* follows:
No beginning, no birth, no death;
All distracting influences at an end;
Steadily persuing the Five *Gati*[3]
Quietly entering into the kalpa of the Three Plagues[4]
O supermost manifestation of wisdom,
Pure essence separated from the gross,
Even though passing through a hundred myriad *kalpas,*
Thou wouldst still be removed far from the dust of this earth.

Thus with the most fitting of my poor language did I strive to glorify the Great Doctrine, measuring, as it were, with the eye of a mosquito, the vast expanse of sky, perceiving not the magnitude of my task, but anxious only to give expression to my heart's burden. And now I take these hymns on the Triple Body, consummate in its excellence, and cause them to be engraved, the hope that prosperity and long life may thereby accrue to

1 The wheel (of the law of Buddha).
2 A great period of time.
3 Conditions of living creatures generally enumerated as six in all.
4 Pestilence, war, and famine.

my honoured Prince, the Sovereign of the Great Sung Empire. For His Majesty is humbly desirous that the destiny of the Doctrine may resemble that of the Sacred Pool, from which nothing may be taken, and to which nothing may be added, the waves of which are liable neither to increase nor decrease; its blessedness that of the Celestial Hill, enduring in majestic loftiness. Still more does my Prince desire that in the future of this kingdom shrine may be added to shrine, and that in other lands and other ages name upon name may be enrolled among the legions of the faithful. Also that others may hymn the praise of the miraculous foot print, and cause the same to be similarly voted down and put on record.

Recorded, and set up in token thereof, this *Jen-hsu* year of the reign of Divine, Favour of the Great Sung' Empire (AD 1021).'[1]

In a postscript the priest Yun-shu adds the following:

There went with me to worship in the land of Buddha the two priests I-ching and I-lin, from the monastery of *Established Doctrine* in the High Street of the Eastern Capital, who each took with him a gold embroidered *Kaśhaya* to be hung up in the shrine of Mahabodhi, and each set up his own memorial tablet in perpetual remembrance thereof."

This long Chinese inscription of Yun-shu was not found at the spot mentioned in the hymn, namely, at 30 paus, or 75 feet, to the north of the Bodhi Tree, but at some distance to eastward, where it was discovered under the foundations of the Såmadh of a Mahant. This inscription is now preserved in the Indian Museum, Calcutta.

(vii) I-ching and I-lin

The two monks *I-ching* and *I-lin,* referred to in the post-script by Yun-shu, have also left behind their own inscription. It reads as:

"We, the Buddhist priest *I-ching* and the novice *I-lin,* from the monastery of 'Doctrine Established,' in the Eastern Capital of the Great Sung Empire, in humble recognition of the Four Mercies and the Three States of Existence, here present one gold-embroidered *Kashaya* to be spread over the throne of the Buddha of the Western Heaven. And we have further caused to be erected a stone Stupa.

Recorded on a day of 4th moon of the 6th year of Divine Favour, when the Upadhya *Pien-cheng* was Chief Teacher."

1 The name of the Imperial House which at that date swayed the destinies of China.

(viii) Yu-pin

Yet another monk in this group, *Yu-pin*, has also left behind his own inscription. He says:

"I, the Buddhist priest *Yu-pin*, from the monastery of the Commencement of Holiness, in the Eastern Capital of the Great Sung Empire, do here present one gold-embroidered *Kashaya* to be spread over the throne of Buddha. And I have further caused to be erected a stone Stupa, in humble recognition of the 'Four Mercies,' and the 'Three States of Existence,' of which I have been mercifully permitted to partake.

Recorded on a day of the 4th moon of the 6th year of Divine Favour.

Both the inscriptions of *I-ching* and *Yu-pin* were actually found in *situ* on two slabs forming the lower part of the basement of two small stupas built of sandstone. These are now preserved in the Indian Museum, Calcutta.

(ix) Hui-wen

Yet another Chinese pilgrim who came in the eleventh century was *Hui-wen.* He came to Buddha Gaya by command of His Imperial Majesty of the Great Sung dynasty to erect a stupa in the honour of the second emperor of that dynasty (AD 976-998). *Hui-wen's* inscription dated in AD 1033 reads as:

"This Stupa was erected by the Emperor and Empress of the Great Sung dynasty, in memory of His Imperial Majesty T, ai Tsung."

"By command of His Imperial Majesty, our divinely enlightened, most glorious, most virtuous, most filial, sovereign of this the Great Sung dynasty, and of Her Imperial Majesty, our most gracious, most virtuous, and most compassionate Empress, I the Buddhist priest, *Hui-wen,* have been humbly commissioned to proceed to the country of Magadha, and to erect, on behalf of His departed Imperial Majesty T'ai Tsung—the humane, the orthodox, the deserving, the divinely virtuous, the wise, the supremely filial—a pagoda beside the Bodhimanda, the Diamond Throne. For His Imperial Majesty, T'ai Tsung, was humbly desirous of passing aloft to the Devaloka, the Mansions of the Blest, there to receive the Word from Buddha himself, to witness the ranks of the Immortal Saints, and be enrolled for ever among the ranks of the faithful; hoping thus to secure to the House of Sung divine protection through all generations."

Recorded this 19th day of the Ist moon of the 2nd year of Ming Tao."

This inscription was discovered by Cunningham concealed under numerous coats of whitewash in the wall of one of the buildings of the Mahant's residence.

When Buddhism declined in India, the flow of the Chinese pilgrims to India also came to a stand-still. And no inscriptional evidence of any visit after the eleventh century has been found at Buddha Gaya.

NOTE

1. All the Chinese inscriptions given here are as presented by Alexander Cunningham, Mahabodhi or the Great Buddhist Temple under the Bodhi Tree at Buddha Gaya, London, 1892, pp. 68-72.

Chapter VI

VISHNUPADA OR BUDDHAPADA?

The disappearance of Buddhism from India, the land of its birth, development and highest achievements, is the most surprising and painful phenomena. How and why the religion of the Buddha lost hold over its original adherents is such a perplexing problem that no two opinions agree. In our opinion, Buddhism in India died an unnatural death and the reasons which led to its disappearance from the land of its birth were external rather than internal. Not only that, a systematic campaign had been launched by certain vested interests to oust Buddhism from its original home.

One of the staunchest opponents of Buddhism was Kumarila Bhatt, a Brahmin. He appears to have lived in the eighth century AD. At his instance, Suddhanvan, the king of Ujjain, is said to have exterminated the Buddhists. The ruthless persecution of the Buddhists by Suddhanvan, at the instigation of Kumarila Bhatt, is recorded in two biographies of Sankaracarya, that is, the Sankaravijaya by Anandagiri, a direct disciple of Sankaracarya, and Sankara-digvijayam by Madhava (fourteenth century AD). In fact, Madhava Acharya asserts that, at the instigation of Kumarila Bhatt, Suddhanvan "Issued orders to put to death all the Buddhists from Ramesvaram to the Himalayas. He further ordered that any one who does not kill a Buddhist would be slain."

Sankaracarya, the Vedanta teacher, was also responsible for the persecution of Buddhists. In fact, he struck a terror into the hearts of the Buddhists. According to a Tibetan tradition, at his approach, "the Buddhists in the monasteries began to disperse pell-mell." He himself says

What was the modus operandi adopted by the Hindus to oust Buddhism from the land of its birth is well illustrated by the legend of Gaya Asura which is recorded in the Gaya Mahatmya, the concluding portion of the Vayu Purana (Chap. 105-112). According to this legend, Gaya-Asura (demon) had attained holiness to such an extent that all who saw or touched him went to heaven. Yama, the lord of hell, grew jealous, and appealed to the gods to limit Gaya Asura's powers. The gods thereupon waited upon Gaya and begged him to grant his pure and holy body for performing a sacrifice. To this, Gaya assented and lay down with his head resting where the old town of Gaya is. The gods then placed a rock over his bead. But this proved insufficient to keep him quiet. Ultimately, Gaya Asura became motionless when Lord Vishnu himself sat upon the stone to prevent its moving, and also promised that the rock over his head will be declared the holiest spot on earth; the devas would rest on that stone; the place would be named as Gaya-Kshetra; and that whoever offered funeral cakes and performed funeral ceremonies would earn merit himself and transmit his ancestors to the heaven, the region of Brahma.

How old is the legend of Gaya Asura is rather difficult to say. Whatever may be the claims of the orthodox Hindus about the antiquity of Gaya, there is sufficient evidence to show that the city of Gaya was elevated to its present status in the Hindu world only after the downfall of Buddhism in India.

In the opinion of Dr. Rajindralal Mitra, a scholar with rare historical insight, the incredible legend related in the Vayu Purana contains an allegory of the final victory of Brahmanism over Buddhism which had flourished strongly in and around Gaya for many centuries. To quote his own words (Buddha Gaya: The Great Buddhist Temple: The Hermitage of Sakya Muni):

> "The Hindus believe this story to the literally true, but Dr. Buchanan calls it "a monstrous legend' and well it may. At first sight nothing can appear more absurd and stupid than this story; it offends every sense of propriety. And has not even the merit of ingenuity in its narration. The Brahmayoni Hill, which is the same with Kalahala Mountain, is scarcely three miles in length, and the idea of locating on it a being 125 yojanas or 576 miles in height and 268 miles in girth would never struck the poorest faller. A head a mile in circumference on a body of 576 miles would bear to each other about the same relation which a pin's head would to the

ordinary human body. The helplessness of the gods to keep down a prostrate monster and their futile attempts to prevent him moving, are as childish as possible. And such being the case, the question suggests itself. How is it that the author of the Vayu Purana of which the Gaya Mahatmya professes to be a part, invented so puerile a story for ensuring the respect and devotion of the people at large to this place? He was not wanting in intelligence, for he discusses many abstruse questions of philosophy with considerable tact and ingenuity. It would be illogical and untrue to say that he could not distinguish the reasonable from the puerile and absurd. To reject, therefore, the story as absurd would in my mind, appear hasty, and indicative of idle impatience. It would much more become the philosophic historian to assume that something esoteric is hidden under the garb of an extravagant fable; and that esoteric meaning. I believe, it is easily found, if the legend be taken as allegory of the success of Brahmanism over Buddhism.''

''Gaya is called an Asura, which ordinarily means A Titan, a demon, a vicious monster, a reviler of gods and religion; but he has not been portrayed as such. He revels not in crime, he injures none, and offends neither the god nor religion by word or deed. On the contrary, he is described as a devout Vaishnava (Stresthah Vaishnavah) who devoted himself to rigorous penance, to long protracted meditations, and to the acquirement of the highest purity of body and soul; one whose very touch sufficed to cleanse mankind of the greatest sin, and to translate them to heaven. The most serious charge brought against him was that he made salvation too simple and summary. The epithet in his case can, therefore, only mean that he did not profess the faith of the Brahmans, nor follow their ways, in short he was a heretic. This character has always been assigned to the chief amongst the Buddhists. They were pious, they were self-mortifying, they devoted themselves greatly to penance and meditation; but they did away with the sacrifices and ceremonies of the Brahmans, and the Gaya therefore may safely be taken to be a personification of Buddhism. His body measured 576 x 268 miles, and the country from Kalinga to the Himalaya, and from Central India to Bengal— the area over which Buddhism had spread at the time when the legend was written—covered fully that space, and a great deal more. The headquarters of Buddhism were then at Gaya; and the town of Gaya is even now barely a mile in extent. The attempt of the gods to put down the head of the monster typifies the attempts of the Hindus to assail Buddhism at its inspiring centre, the headquarters; and the thwack of Vishnu's mace indicates the resort which had been made to force when religious preaching had failed to attain the end. The rock of religion was placed on the head of the infidel, and the force of the gods kept it fixed and immovable. It was the blessing of the gods, too, which sanctified the seat of Buddhism into a principal sanctuary of the Ḥindu faith. We are well aware of the means resorted to at Puri, Bhuvanesvar, and elsewhere to render Buddhist emblems. Buddhist shrines, and even Buddhist idols subservient to Hindu worship, and it would not be at all unreasonable to suppose that the same process had been resorted to at Gaya." (Mitra, Buddha Gaya 1878; 14-18).

The royal and religious persecution apart, the Hindus also reformed their systems to fall in line with the Buddhist practices which were popular with the masses. Not only that, they also appropriated the Buddhist shrines in due course and replaced the Buddhist images with those of Hindu gods and goddesses. The important Buddhist shrines which met this fate include the Great Maha Bodhi Temple at Buddha Gaya as well. The Seat of Buddha's Enlightenment was in the possession of a Hindu Mahant till 1952. Similarly, at Kushinara, where the Buddha had entered into Mahaparinirvana, the cremation stupa had been converted into a Hindu temple, and on the top of it stood the temple of Rāmbhar Bhavani when Cunningham discovered the site in 1860-61. Among the shrines which still continue to be dedicated to the Hindu gods, mention may be made of the Caityas of Chezrala and Ter in Andhra Pradesh which are now Siva and Vishnu temples respectively. The temple of Madhava at Sal Kusa, opposite Gauhati in Assam, was once a sacred shrine of the Buddhists. Sankaracharya is also said to have founded his Sringeri Math (Karnataka) on the site of a Buddhist monastery. And the famous Jagannatha temple at Puri in Orissa was also originally a Buddhist shrine. Similarly, the Vishnupada temple at Gaya was also once a Buddhist shrine.

Gaya was visited atleast twice by Lord Buddha — Once on His way from Rajagriha to Uruvela, and again on His return from Sarnath, immediately after turning the Wheel of Law (Dharma-Chakra pravartana). On the second occasion, the Blessed One had also delivered a sermon on 'burning fire of passions (Aditta-Pariyaya-Sutta-Samyutta-Nikaya XXXV, 28) while camping on the Gaya-sirsa hill. Therefore, as Buddhism spread in India and the flow of pilgrims to Buddha Gaya, the

Seat of Buddha's Enlightenment, increased, several shrines came up at Gaya. One of them was on the spot where the Buddha had first set His foot after crossing the river Neranjara (Falgu) while coming to Gaya from Rajagriha. Another stood on the Gayasirsa hill where the Buddha had delivered 'the fire sermon.' The third one was on the place where the Kasyapa brothers (Gaya Kasyapa, Nadi Kasyapa and Uruvela Kasyapa) were born. In the seventh century AD when Hiuen Tsang visited Gaya, he saw three massive stupas on the above noted places. Of them, the stupa enshrining the footprint of the Buddha was particularly the Chief object of worship with the pious devotees in and around Gaya.

The city of Gaya is at present an important place of pilgrimage for the Hindus. It has numerous sacred centres — temples, trees, tanks, rivers and hills — where the Shraddha sacrificers are enjoined to offer funeral cakes in memorium to their dead ancestors. Of all the sacred spots in the Gaya Kshetra, the temple of Vishnupada, situated on the bank of the river Falgu, is the most famous shrine. It is said to mark the place where Lord Vishnu placed his foot on the head of the demon Gaya, and made him motionless. Though for long the footprints in the Vishnupada temple have been treated and venerated by the Hindus as the legendary feet of Vishnu, yet in reality it is not so. The foot-prints in the Vishnupada are the foot-prints of Lord Buddha, and were appropriated by the Hindus after the downfall of Buddhism in Gaya and around. Apparently, this was done by the clever Brahmin priests to win over the masses as says Dr. Rajendralal Mitra:

> "Next to Chaityas, the most important object was the impression of the Buddha's feet. In fact it was the first to come into worship, and only veneration was shown to the relics of the great reformer. In later days, however, when the images of the last Buddha became popular, the feet which constituted only a part thereof, fell to the background. But they were never altogether given up, and in all Buddhist countries carving of Buddha's feet are held in great veneration. In many temples they occupy the most prominent place; and when the Hindus got hold of Gaya, the popular feeling in favour of the most sacred foot-print there was so high that unable to set it aside, the Brahmans recognised it under the name of Vishnu's feet, as the most-sacred object of worship at the place." (Mitra, Buddha Gaya: 174).

The foot-print in the Vishnupada temple, which was rebuilt in the closing years of the eighteenth century by Ahilya Bai Holkar, a Maratha queen, is engraved in the basalt. Now there are no distinguishing marks on it as centuries of washing and scrubbing have obliterated the usual Buddhist symbols. In spite of that, it is truism to say that the foot-print in the Vishnupada was originally a Buddhist emblem which was appropriated by the Hindu priests, after the decline of Buddhism. The following conclusive evidence will prove our point:

(i) The Buddha's footprints were carved on stone and served as an object of veneration at many Buddhist shrines as early as the second century BC. In the sculptures of Bharhut (in Madhya Pradesh) we find that "on the bas-relief representing Ajatasatru's homage to the Lord are visible two footprints marked by a wheel, and symbolically indicating the presence of the Lord. The footprints of the Buddha were also a popular object of veneration in South India. And this is much before Vishnu's footprint is found at any Hindu site.

(ii) The city of Gaya was elevated to its present status in the Hindu world only after the downfall of Buddhism in India. Nothing much is known about its history before the eighth or ninth century, nor of its earlier monuments.

(iii) In order to make the Hinduised Gaya popular with the masses and to create a halo around its sanctity, the Hindus had to invent the fantastic and incredible legend of Gaya Asura.

(iv) Nowhere else in India has the worship of footprints received such a high place and honour in the cult of Hindus.

(v) The fact that the Vishnupada was once a Buddhist shrine has also been confirmed by the findings of L.P. Vidyarthi, who carried out extensive field researches at Gaya in 1951-1956. He says in The Sacred Complex in Hindu Gaya as follows:

> "Another important feature at some of the sacred clusters is reflected in the appropriation of Buddhistic images and emblems as Hindu deities. Mitra (1878:124-6) considers with all confidence that the mark of Vishnu's foot enshrined in the Vishnupada temple was originally a Buddhist emblem which was appropriated by the Hindu priests at the time of the conversion of Gaya to Hinduism. General Cunningham (1871: 9-10) lends further support to this view. However, to the thousands of pilgrims who come every year from different parts of India, it symbolizes the legendary foot of Lord Vishnu. They in no way have the slightest association with Buddha at the time of worshipping it and they never identify it with Bud-

dhism. It is a commonplace sight to see Buddhistic images in many of the verandas or wall-shelves of the temples, or under the trees, or near the sacred ghats. These images, however, are not identified with Buddha and are worshipped by the ignorant and devoted Hindus as their own gods and goddesses." (Vidyarthi" 23-24)

Yet another fact which supports our view is that the Gayawals, priests of the Vishnupada temple complex, in the opinion of some scholars are the descendants of the Buddhist monks who were converted by Sankaracarya to the faith of Hinduism and persuaded to act as shraddha priests under the name of Gayawal. "Sankaracarya is said to have visited Gaya during his great religious conquest over Buddhism (Kashyapa 1952: Vidyarthi: 1954). He is believed to have had a great part in establishing the importance of Gaya as a place of pilgrimage for shraddha sacrifice. He is also said to have converted the Buddhist monks to the Hindu priesthood and popularized them throughout India under the name of Gayawal during his tour of religious conquest, popularly known as Sankara Digvijaya. Recently a park, along with his image, has been installed in memory of his historic visit to Gaya. The desolate math with hundreds of Sanskrit books also reminds us that Sankara had great influence at Gaya. There are numerous priests and householders who consider themselves to be followers of Sankara (Vidyarthi: 68).

Significantly enough, the Gayawals, having no lineage within the Hindu caste-structure, claim themselves to have been specially created by the Brahma to act as shraddha priests at Gaya. "All the Gayawal," says Vidyarthi "are united by the same mythology which explains their single common origin by the hands of Brahma into fourteen clans (gotra). The purpose of their creation, it is said, was to assist Brahma in the performance of the great sacrifice that followed the killing of the holy demon Gaya Asur. The Vayu Purana which celebrates the mythology of Gaya Asur also sanctions the respect and worship of the Gayawal priests, especially by the shraddha sacrificers." (Ibid, p. 53)

The Hindus even adopted the Bodhi Tree and enjoined that the pilgrims before offering the funeral cakes at Vishnupada should go to Buddha Gaya and salute the Bodhi Tree. In the Gaya Mahatmya (Vayu Purana) even a special mantra has been provided for saluting the Bodhi Tree. It says:

> "I salute, thee, repeatedly salute, Aswattha tree, the tremendous leaved, the yajna (sacrifice personified), the Bodhisattva, the eternal source of permanence. . .O noble Pipal tree, since Narayana

always reside within thee, therefore, are thou the most beneficient among the trees." (Chap. III, 24-27 and 80).

With regard to the absorption of the Bodhi Tree by the Hindus, Vidyarthi remarks:

> "With regard to the Bodhi Tree under which Buddha is said to have got Enlightenment, the process of absorption by Hinduism is neither complete nor free from conflict. The Bodhi Tree has a definite association with Buddhism as it is located right at the back of the temple of Buddha in the sacred zone of Buddha Gaya. It is also one of the sacred centres which the shraddha sacrificers visit on the fourth day of their rounds. The latter appears to be a case of appropriation as an object of adoration by the Hindus. When it was so appropriated we have no means of knowing; but it seems certain that it was an object of worship by the Hindus as early as the seventh century AD, for about AD 600 Sasanka, a devoted adherent of Brahmanism, dug it up and burnt it with fire "desiring," as Hiuen Tsang says "to destroy it utterly and not leave trace of it behind" (Hiuen T sang AD 629: Bk. VIII, 117-8). It appears probable that the Brahman priests might have adopted the tree as a suitable object of veneration on the decline of Buddhism and in this way made profitable use of the worship it received from the Buddhists. In Vayu Purana (Chap. lll, vss. 24-27, 80) its worship is highly celebrated and special invocations are given for it. Buchanan also mentions worship being offered to it in 1811, though he goes on to say that some zealous person had lately built a stairway on the side of the terrace "so that the orthodox may pass without entering the porch and thus seeing the hateful image of Buddha." (Vidyarthi: 24-25).

In the light of the evidence marshalled by Vidyarthi, it is truism to say that the Vishnupada temple in the city of Gaya was once a Buddhapada shrine.

Chapter VII

STRUGGLE FOR SURVIVAL

The struggle for survival at Buddha Gaya began at the beginning of the seventh century AD when for the first time a fanatic Hindu king Sasanka, who was a Brahmin by caste and a Saiva by faith, desecrated the Great Maha Bodhi Temple, and in his anger he almost destroyed the Bodhi Tree. Hiuen Tsang, who visited Buddha Gaya in AD 637, about three decades after the incident, records as follows:

> "In late times Sasanka-raja being a believer in heresy, slandered the religion of Buddha, and through envy destroyed the convents and cut down the Bodhi Tree, digging it up to the very springs of the earth; but yet he did not get to the bottom of the roots. Then he burnt with fire and sprinkled it with the juice of the sugarcane, desiring to destroy it entirely, and not leave a trace of it behind." (Samuel Beal, Buddhist Records of the Western World: vol. ii, p. II8).

According to Hiuen Tsang, the king Sasanka also wanted to destroy the most venerated image of the Buddha in the Maha Bodhi Temple. He says:

> "Sasanka-raja, having cut down the Bodhi tree, wished to destroy this image; but having seen its loving features, his mind had no rest or determination, and he returned with his retinue homewards. On his way he said to one of his officers, "We must remove that statue of Buddha and place there a figure of Mahesvara." The officer having received the order, was moved with fear, and, sighing, said, "If I destroy the figure of Buddha, then during successive kalpas I shall reap misfortune; if I disobey the king, he will put me to a cruel death and destroy my family; in either case, whether I obey or disobey, such will be the consequences; what, then, shall I do?"

On this he called to his presence a man with a believing heart (i.e., a believer in Buddha) to help him, and sent him to build up across the chamber and before the figure of Buddha a wall of brick. The man, from a feeling of shame at the darkness, placed a burning lamp (with the concealed figure); then on the interposing wall he drew a figure of (or, he made a figure of) Mahesvara-deva." (Ibid., pp.ii, 121-122)

Hiuen Tsang further reports that the concerned officer, after constructing an intervening wall to conceal the Buddha image, reported the matter to the king. And as soon as this was done, the king suffered immediate grave consequences for having ordered desecration of the sacred Bodhi Tree and the Buddha image, and died of a deadly disease.

The cutting of the sacred Bo-Tree by Sasanka sent shock waves among the Buddhists in general, and Raja Purna Varma, the last descendant of Asoka in Magadha, in particular. He took immediate steps to restore the Bodhi Tree. To quote Hiuen Tsang again:

" Some months afterwards, the king of Magadha, called Purnavarma (*Pu-la-na-fa-mo*), the last of the race of Asoka-raja, hearing of it, sighed and said, "The sun of wisdom having set, nothing is left but the tree of Buddha, and this they have now destroyed, what source of spiritual life is there now?" He then cast his body on the ground overcome with pity; then with the milk of a thousand cows he again bathed the roots of the tree, and in a night it once again revived and grew to the height of some 10 feet. Fearing lest it should be again cut down, he surrounded it with a wall of stone 24 feet high. So the tree is now encircled with a wall about 20 feet high." (Ibid., ii.p. 118)

Towards the middle of the eighth century AD, Buddha Gaya came under the Pala kings who were Buddhists and ruled in Eastern India for the longest period of over 400 years from 750 onwards. The founder of the Pala dynasty was Gopala Deva, who ruled from 750 to 776 AD. An inscription discovered at Buddha Gaya records the dedication of a Buddha statue there during his reign.

Gopala was succeeded by his son, Dharmapala. He ruled from 766-810 AD, and was a great patron of the Nalanda Mahavihara (University). He also founded the well-known Vikramasila Mahavihara, near Bhagalpur. But he does not appear to have done any pious act at the holy Seat of Buddha's Enlightenment. On the contrary, it was during his reign that a four-faced image of Siva (Chaumukh-Mahadeva) was installed at

Bodh Gaya by Kesava, son of Ujjavala, the stone-cutter, for the benefit of the Brahmin inhabitants of the town. A nine-line inscription in Sanskrit dated in the 26th year of the reign of Dharmapala is now preserved in the Indian Museum, Calcutta. Besides the inscription, it shows three figures of Surya, Siva and Vishnu. (B.M. Barua, Gaya and Buddha Gaya: pp. 231-232.)

Two Buddhistic inscriptions of this period have also been found at Buddha Gaya. One of them tells us "that the Buddhist king Sri Purnabhadra of Sindh erected a Gandhakuti (temple) at Buddha Gaya installing three Buddha images therein and another Gandhakuti was erected, "Like unto a flight of steps into heaven," by king Tunga of the Rashtrakuta family in the 15th year of his reign."

Dharmapala was succeeded by his worthy son, Devapala. He ruled from 820-850 AD. He was also a great patron of Buddhism, as also of the Nalanda University. It was during his reign that Balaputradeva, a king of the Sailendra dynasty of the kingdom of Srivijaya in Sumatra, had sent a mission asking for a grant of five villages for the upkeep of the monastery built by him at Nalanda. Devapala granted his request.

Mahipala I, the ninth Pala king, was the last great Pala King who ruled for fifty years from 980-1030 AD over the vast Pala empire. According to an inscription discovered at Bodh Gaya, Mahipala I carried out repairs to the Maha Bodhi Temple in the 10th year of his reign. The pious Mahipala is eulogised in the inscription as a '*Parama-Bhattaraka Parama-Saugata, Sriman Mahipala-deva*,' "the supreme sovereign, the pre-eminent Buddhist, the fortunate Mahipala-deva." (Cunningham: Maha Bodhi: 65).

By the time of Mahipala I (980-1030 AD), the Vikramasila Mahavihara, founded by Dharmapala (776-810 AD) had become a great centre of learning, and had as many as 108 highly qualified teachers. The head of Vikramasila at that time was Jnanasrimitra, a great saint-scholar of Buddhism. According to Taranatha, the Maha Bodhi Temple was saved from being destroyed by fire because of Jnanasrimitra's timely action. The Tibetan historian says:

> "Once, while he (Jnanasrimitra) was residing in Vikrama(sila), he told a novice monk, 'start immediately so that you can reach the city of Gaya by tomorrow noon. A Brahmana has invited there all the monks with the priests incharge of the temple of Vajrasana to a seasonal feast. The Gandola containing the

Mahabodhi will be damaged by fire. Take them along to put the fire out.'

He went to Gaya and, as predicted, met the residents of Vajrasana. He said, 'My guru has predicted thus. So please return (to Vajrasana).' Half of them did not believe him and stayed back.

When he reached Vajrasana with the other half of them, the Gandola of Vajrasana had already caught fire. Both the interior and the exterior were aflame. They extinguished the fire with prayer to the deity and thus the temple was saved from further damage. The acarya arranged for the restoration of the damaged paintings and the renovation of the wooden structure." (Taranatha's History of Buddhism in India; pp.302-303.)

Incidentally, Atisa (Dipankara Srijnana) (982-1054 AD), who later played a major role in the resurgence of Buddhism in Tibet, had studied Vinaya for two years at a monstery at Buddha Gaya. Born as a prince in 982, he became a sramanera at the age of eleven under Bhikkhu Bodhibhadra, the then head of the Nalanda Mahavihara. From Nalanda, he came to Vikramasila, and learnt the cult of mantra for eleven years under Naropa, a great scholar and a Siddha. Even after completing his studies at Nalanda and Vikramasila, Atisa's thirst for knowledge was not quenched. So he came to Buddha Gaya in 1011 and became a disciple of Mahavinayadhara Silarakshita of Mativihara, and studied the Vinayapitaka under him for two years.

The famous Tiberan translator, Rinchen bzangpo (958-1055) had also come to Buddha Gaya to complete his studies which he had begun in Kashmir.

Mahipala I was succeeded by Nayapala, who ruled from 1030 to 1050 AD. He too patronised Vajrasana (Buddha Gaya) and Vikramasila as well as the great Buddhist scholars like Jnanasrimitra, Jetari and Dipankara Srijnana.

Nayapala was succeeded by Vigrahapala III, who ruled from 1050 to 1076 AD. An inscribed Buddha image of 12th year of his reign was discovered from Bihar-sharief in the Nalanda district. Vigrahapala III was succeeded by his elder son, Mahipala II, but his reign was short-lived. Then came Rampala, his younger brother, who ruled for a long period of 53 years or according to some scholars for 42 years, and died in 1132 AD. About the status of Buddhism in Magadha during the reign of Rampala, Taranatha says:

"Though he ascended the throne at an early age, he extended his power widely by virtue of his exceptional intelligence.

Shortly after he became king, the great acarya Abhayakaragupta was invited to act as the Upadhyaya of Vajrasana. After many years, he was appointed as the Upadhyaya of Vikramasila and Nalanda. By this time, the older tradition of these centres had changed.

One hundred and sixty panditas and about a thousand monks permanently resided in Vikramasila. Even five thousand ordained monks assembled there for occasional offerings. In Vajrasana forty Mahayanis and two hundred Sravaka bhikkhus were maintained by the king as the permanent residents. Occasionally even ten thousand Sravaka monks congregated there. In Odantapuri also permanently lived a thousand monks belonging to both Hinayana and Mahayana. Occasionally even twelve thousand monks congregated there." (Taranatha's History of Buddhism in India: 303.)

The Pala dynasty collapsed within thirty years of Rampala's death and all was over by 1162. In Bengal, the Palas were overthrown by the Senas, a new rising power. The most powerful king of this dynasty was Lakshmanasena. Opinions differ in regard to his ascending the throne. Some scholars take the date as 1118-1119 while Cunningham determines it as 1106. Lakshmanasena had begun his own era, and there are atleast two inscriptions at Bodh Gaya which are dated in the Lakshmanasena era. These inscriptions are that of Raja Asoka-balla of Sapdalksha (Siwalik Hills) in the Punjab, who had carried out major repairs to the Maha Bodhi Temple in response to a specific request by the Bhikkhu Sangha of Buddha Gaya. The third inscription dated in the year 1813 of the Buddha era clearly says that the king Asoka-balla, with the assistance of a local chief named Purusottama Simha, built a Gandhakuti or the Temple of the Buddha, and carried out several works of repair and renovation under the superintendence of a Buddhist monk called Dharmarakshita. Another inscription dated in the year 51 of the era of Lakshmanasena of Bengal, or in AD 1106 + 57 = 1157, of the King Asoka-balla and found at Buddha Gaya says:

"Adoration to Buddha. The Great Sramana. He it is who tells what the root is from which virtue springs, as also what it is that chokes that virtue. This is the virtuous gift of the great King, the illustrious Asoka-balla Deva, and adherent of the excellent Mahayana School, a great Upasaka, pious at heart. May whatever be its merit, be for the advancement in spiritual knowledge, first of my father and mother, and after them of all beings." (Cunningham, Mahabodhi: p.78.)

By the time of Asoka-balla, it seems the responsibility for looking after the Puja ceremonies at the sacred Buddha Gaya shrine had been completely taken over by the venerable monks from Sri Lanka, in the absence of the Indian Bhikkhus. In the second part of the same inscription, Asoka-balla says:

"Moreover for the offering to Buddha, the daily ration with pots, incense and lamps, shall be given so long as the Sun and Moon shall endure by the leaders of Lanka Assembly in Mahabodhi."

(Cunningham, Mahabodhi: p. 79.)

According to Taranatha, the eighty year rule of the Senas in Magadha was marked by the sudden decline of Buddhism in Magadha. He says:

"During the time of these four Senas, the number of tirthika-s went on increasing even in Magadha. There also came many Persian followers of the mleccha view. To protect Odantapuri and Vikramasila, the king even converted these partially into fortresses and stationed some soldiers there. The Mahayanis did not have any special importance in Vajrasana, though some of the yogis and Mahayanis continued to preach there."

(Taranatha's History of Buddhism in India: p. 309.)

The fate of Buddha Gaya, rather Buddhism and all the Buddhist shrines in Bihar, was sealed when in AD 1197 Allauddin Khilji sacked Nalanda and massacred all the Buddhist monks residing therein. Commenting on the Muslim onslaught, Dr. B.R. Ambedkar says:

"The Muslim invasions of India commenced in the year 1001 AD. The last wave of these invasions reached Southern India in 1296 AD when Allauddin Khilji subjugated the Kingdom of Devagiri. The Muslim conquest of India was really not completed by 1296. The wars of subjugation went on between the Muslim conquerors and the local rulers who though defeated were not reduced. But the point which requires to bear in mind is that during this period of 300 years of Muslim Wars of conquests, India was governed all over by princes who professed the orthodox faith of Brahmanism. Brahmanism beaten and battered by the Muslim Invaders could look to the rulers for support and sustenance and did get it. Buddhism beaten and battered by the Muslim invaders had no such hope. It was an unearned for orphan and it withered in the cold blast of the native rulers and was consumed in the fire lit up by the conquerors.

The Musalman invaders sacked the Buddhist Universities of Nalanda, Vikramasila, Jagaddala, Odantapuri to name only a few. They raised to the ground Buddhist monasteries with which the country was studded. The Monks fled away in thousands to Nepal, Tibet and other places outside India. A very large number were killed outright by the Muslim commanders. How the Buddhist priesthood perished by the sword of the Muslim invaders has been recorded by the Muslim historians themselves. Summarizing the evidence relating to the slaughter of the Buddhist Monks perpetrated by the Musalman General in the course of his invasion of Bihar in 1197 AD. Vincent Smith says:

"The Musalman General, who had already made his name a terror by repeated plundering expeditions in Bihar, seized the capital by a daring stroke. The almost contemporary historian met one of the survivors of the attacking party in AD 1243, and learned from him that the Fort of Bihar was seized by a party of only two hundred horsemen, who boldly rushed to the eastern gate and gained possession of the place. Great quantities of plunder were obtained and the slaughter of the 'shaven headed Brahmans,' that is to say the Buddhist monks, was so thoroughly completed, that when the victor sought for some one capable of explaining the contents of the books in the libraries of the monasteries, not a living man could be found who was able to read them. 'It was discovered,' we are told, 'that the whole of that fortress and city was a college, and in the Hindi tongue they call a college Bihar."

Such was the slaughter of the Buddhist priesthood perpetrated by the Islamic invaders. The axe was struck at the very root. For by killing the Buddhist priesthood Islam killed Buddhism. This was the greatest disaster that befell the religion of Buddha in India. Religion like any other ideology can be sustained only by propaganda. If propaganda fails, religion must disappear. The priestly class, however detestable it may be, is necessary to the sustenance of religion. For it is by its propaganda that religion is kept up. Without the priestly class religion must disappear. The sword of Islam fell heavily upon the priestly class. It perished or it fled outside India. Nobody remained to keep the flame of Buddhism burning." (B.R. Ambedkar, Writings and Speeches, Vol.III: pp. 232-233.)

The Great Maha Bodhi Temple luckily escaped destruction but was subjected to sacrilege, and was practically deserted by the Buddhists from fear of Turkish soldiery who had created terror in the area. What happened to the sacred shrine at that time is vividly told by Dharmasvamin, a Tibetan pilgrim, who was in Buddha Gaya in AD 1234. Giving an eye-witness account, he says:

> "The place was deserted and only four monks were found staying (in the Vihara). One (of them) said, "It is not good! All have fled from fear of the Turushka soldiery." They blocked up the door in front of the Mahabodhi image with bricks and plastered it. Near it they placed another image as a substitute. They also plastered the outside door (of the temple). On its surface they drew the image of Mahesvara in order to protect it from Non-Buddhists. The monks said, "We do not dare to remain here and shall have to flee."
>
> "At daybreak, they fled towards the North following the rut of a cart, and for seventeen days he (Dharmasvamin) did not see the face of the image (i.e. the Mahabodhi image). At that time, a woman appeared who brought the welcome news that the Turushka soldiery had gone far away. Then he returned to Vajrasana, and stayed there worshipping and circumambulating the image of Mahabodhi."
>
> (George Roerich, Biography of Dharmasvamin: p. xviii.)
>
> About the Maha Bodhi Temple, Dharmasvamin says:
>
> "The Temple was surmounted by a pinnacle of "glittering white" that "looked like a flame. . . that . . . stone looked like a shield placed flat on the ground in the sunshine." In front of the eastern door, there were three covered passages. Inside, was a large image of the Mahabodhi (Buddha)."
>
> Dharmasvamin adds:
>
> "The Bodhi tree stands inside a fort-like structure surrounded on the south, west and north by a brick wall; it has pointed leaves of bright green colour. Having opened a door one sees a large trench of the shape of a basin. . . The devotees worship (the tree) with curd, milk and perfumes such as sandalwood, camphor and so on. They bring offerings from afar and keep it constantly moist." (Ibid, pp. xxxi-xxxvi).

Soon after Dharmasvamin's visit, the Maha Bodhi Temple was lost into oblivion. It was practically deserted in the following centuries, and became more and more ruinous.

Chapter VIII

BURMA REPAIRS THE MAHA BODHI TEMPLE

As in Sri Lanka, so also in Burma (Myanmar) Buddhism was introduced in the third century BC during the reign of Asoka the Great (BC 273-232). The missionaries who preached the Dhamma in Burma were Sona and Uttara. According to tradition, the Pali scriptures were introduced into Lower Burma by Buddhaghosha, the famous Pali scholar and commentator, who flourished in the fifth century AD. Born near Buddha Gaya, Buddhaghosha was prompted by Ven. Revata, the chief monk of the Buddha Gaya Temple to go to Sri Lanka, where he studied Pali, wrote the Visuddhimagga and the commentaries on the Tripitaka. Buddhaghosha is also said to have translated the Buddhist texts into Burmese. This gave impetus to the development of Buddhism in Burma.

In the following centuries, while Lower Burma adhered to the Theravada form of Buddhism, Upper Burma came under the influence of the Tantric cult and the superstitious Nat-worship. And by the beginning of the eleventh century, the country had reached the lowest ebb of its Tantric phase. Then, a great event took place in the history of Burma. This was the advent of a dynamic king of Pagan, Anawrahta (also spelt as Anawrahta or Anorutha or Anurudha). When Anawrahta came to the throne in 1044, Munuha King of Thaton (Lower Burma) had thirty copies of Tripitaka, written on palm-leaves, while the Upper Burma had no such scriptures. Then in 1056, Shin Arhan, a Bhikkhu from Thaton, came to Pagan with a view to preaching the Dhamma there. He succeeded in converting the king and his courtiers to the Theravada form of Buddhism. Thereupon, Anawrahta asked the King of Thaton for a copy of the Pali Tripitaka but he refused. This enraged Anawrahta. He invaded Thaton; defeated Munuha, and annexed his kingdom to his own Empire. The Tripitakas were brought to Pagan and kept in a library. Anawrahta made

Shin Arahan his Sangha Raja and took steps to spread Theravada Buddhism throughout Burma. The reign of Anawrahta (1044-1077 AD) is considered to be the golden age of Burma. Under this great conqueror and reformer, Burma decidedly for the first time, witnessed political unification and religious purification. As a result, the Theravada Buddhism has endured in Burma to date.

The first serious effort by Burma to repair and restore the Maha Bodhi Temple was made in the eleventh century during the reign of king Kyanzittha, who had been Anawrahta's general, and ruled the Pagan kingdom from 1085-1113. Kyanzittha's mission is mentioned in a Mon inscription from Prome. It says that since the temple of Sri Vajrasana had been destroyed by other kings, Kyanzittha got together jewels of diverse kinds and sent them in a ship to build up the holy temple.

Since the repairs undertaken by Kyanzittha were quite extensive, the work could not be completed during his life time, and as such was completed only in the reign of his immediate successor, king Alaungsithu who ascended the throne in 1113. In this noble task, he was assisted by king Letyminnan, the ruler of Arakan, who had gained his ancestral throne with the assistance of Alaungsithu. According to a Burmese inscription discovered at Buddha Gaya, the supervision of the work was entrusted to Penthagu, son of the lord of Seinnyat.

Another Burmese inscription found near the Bodhi Tree recorded that Mindi, a king of Arakan, also repaired the Maha Bodhi Temple in AD 1296-1298. This ruler of Arakan is reported to have repaired not only the Temple but some other structures as well.

Yet another Burmese inscription discovered by Cunningham on a wall of the Mahant's residence tells us that the Burmese had again undertaken repairs to the Maha Bodhi Temple in the Burmese era 667-668, which would come to AD 1305-1306 (667 + 638 or 668 + 638). The significance of this inscription lies in the fact that it also attempts to give past history of the Temple, beginning from Asoka. There are as many as three translations of this inscription, namely, by Ratna Pala, a Pali scholar of Sri Lanka, Col. Burney, and Hla Oung, a Burmese. For facility of comparison, we reproduce here the first and the third translations, as given by Cunningham (Mahabodhi; 76-77):

Ratna Pala

"This is one of the 84,000 shrines erected by Sri Dharma Asoka, ruler of the world (Jambodwip), at the end of the 218th year of Buddha annihilation (BC 326) upon holy spot in which Bhagwan (Buddha) tasted milk and honey (Madhupayasa). In lapse of time, having fallen into disrepair, it was rebuilt by a priest named Naik-Mahanta. Again, being ruined, it was restored by Raja Sado Mang. After a long interval it was once more demolished, when Raja Sempyu-sakhen-tra-Mengi appointed his guru, Sri Dharma Raja Guna, to superintend the building. He proceeded to the spot with his disciple, Sri Kasyapa, but they were unable to complete it although aided in every way by the Raja. Afterwards Varadasi-naik-thera petitioned the Raja to undertake it, to which he readily assented, commissioning Prince Pyutasing to the work, who again deputed the younger Pyusakheng, and his minister, Ratha, to cross over and repair the sacred building. It was thus constructed a fourth time, and finished on Friday the 10th day of Pyadola, in the Sakkaraj year 667 (AD 1305). On Sunday, the 8th of Tachhaanmungla, 668 (AD 1306), it was consecrated with splendid cremonies and offerings of food, perfumes, banners, and lamps, and pooja of the famous ornamented tree called calpavriksha, and the poor (two ?) were treated with charity, as the Raja's own children. Thus was completed this meritorious act, which will produce reward and virtuous fruits. May the founders endure in fame, enjoy the tranquillity of Nirbhan, and Arhanta on the advent of Arya Maitri (the future Buddha)."

Hla Oung

"Of the 84,000 shrines of the great King Dhamma Asoka, who ruled over Zamboodwip Island, when 218 years had elapsed since the Lord's religion came into existence. Payathabat, a temple built on the spot where Buddha took a meal, having fallen into disrepair by lapse of time, a Pentha-googyee repaired it. When it again fell into disrepair, the lord of the white elephant and king of righteousness, sent, as his representative, his teacher, Sri Dhamma Rajguna, who was accompanied by his disciple, Kathaba Thera. Not being able to perform the work, although he had made money to do it, the lord off the 100,000 Pyoos made a priest, Wardathi, to undertake the work, and spared the lesser lord of the Pyoos and prime minister, Ratha, for it. The work was commenced on Friday the 10th of the waxing moon of the Pyatho month in the year 667, and on Sunday the 8th of the waxing moon of Tazoungmon month in the year 668, offerings were made of pretty flags and kookahs. Offerings of 1,000 thinboots and 1,000 lights were made. Offerings were also made of 21 lads regarded as children of the bosom, and of a Padetha tree suspended with gold and silver flowers, cups, and cloth. And in order that the meal offering may be regularly observed, debtor slaves and cows were purchased and dedicated to the service. It is desired that this meritorious act may be an aid to the attainment of Nirvana, and of a reward of salvation at the time of Arimadeya Buddha."

The five stages of construction/repairs of the Maha Bodhi Temple, as indicated in this inscription would be as follows:

1. Asoka built the first temple.
2. Naik Mahanta rebuilt the temple.
3. The temple was restored by Raja-Sado-Mang.
4. Raja Sempyu-Sahken-tra-Mengi sent his guru Sri Dharmaraja Guna to superintend restoration of the temple, but the work not completed.
5. Varadasi Naik Thera petitioned the king to undertake the work, which was then started in AD 1305 and completed in AD 1306.

According to Cunningham, "the Burmese repairs extended to complete restoration of the whole building, including the rebuilding of the pinnacle, an amount of work which must have occupied several years."

The kings referred to in this inscription must be those belonging to the kingdom of Pagan who were very devoted to the Maha Bodhi Temple. So much so that one of them in the thirteenth century erected an exact replica of the Buddha Gaya Temple in the city of Pagan, and also called it "The Mahabodhi Pagoda". This Mahabodhi temple in Burma is still standing and in good condition.

The kingdom of Pagan began disintegrating in the thirteenth century as a result of the Tartar invasions. Hence, the Burmese ties with the Buddha Gaya Temple were also snapped, and remained so till 1472 when the king of Pegu, Dhammazendi, sent a royal mission to Buddha Gaya with the primary object of taking plans of the historic Maha Bodhi Temple for adopting the same as model for the new Temple at Pegu. And such a temple, called Schwegugyi was indeed built at Pegu in the fifteenth century. Unfortunately, the Schwegugyi in Pegu is now in ruins.

After the visit of this royal mission the Burmese appear to have forgotten the Buddha Temple as there was practically no contact between Burma and the Seat of Buddha's Enlightenment for the next 400 years till we come to the reign of the king Mindon Min of Mandalay in the nineteenth century.

Chapter IX

THE MAHANT AND THE MAHA BODHI TEMPLE

The last scene of the Buddhist drama in the theatre of its homeland,'' as a writer puts it, ''began in terror and ended in silence, the silence of the forgotten. The holy places fell into decay, overgrown by jungle, their shrines converted to another faith.'' The Great Maha Bodhi Temple was no exception. After the fall of Buddhism in Magadha, it was practically deserted by the Buddhists, and the flow of pilgrims to Buddha Gaya came to a standstill. Barring the arrival of royal missions from Myanmar (Burma) which primarily came with a view to repairing the Temple, there were hardly any visitors from abroad. And from within the country, only some pilgrims came from Sind and Punjab in the 14th and 15th century respectively, and left records of their visits by way of brief inscriptions. Thereafter, the holiest of the holy Buddhist shrine was completely forgotten, and lost into oblivion.

Nothing is known about the Maha Bodhi Temple for the next two hundred years till in 1590 a Hindu Saiva Mahant, Gosain Ghamandi Giri, tumbled upon it, and finding the place secluded and peaceful, decided to make it his permanent abode. Accordingly, he built a small monastery near the Great Temple. The Mahant's monastery began to grow fast when Ghamandi Giri's successor, Mahant Lala Giri acquired the vast land around the villages of Mastipur and Taradih which were given to him as grants by the Moghul Emperor of Delhi. In the firman of the Muslim ruler, however, there was no mention of the Maha Bodhi Temple as the same was in the village of Bodh Gaya, and not in the villages granted. Later sometime in the eighteenth century, a successor of Ghamandi Giri, Dhamandinatha Giri, occupied the Maha Bodhi Temple Complex itself. As there were no Buddhists around the occupation of the Buddhist shrine by a Hindu Mahant raised no eye-brows. Dhamandinatha was followed by Chaitanya Giri, who was followed by his disciple Mahadeva. It was during this time that the sacrilege of the Great Buddhist Temple began. As a first step, the courtyard of the Temple, where stood hundreds of stupas, chaityas, small shrines with Buddha images, was turned into a graveyard. The first Mahant to be buried near the eastern gate of the Great Temple was Chaitanya Giri. Later, two other Mahants, Mahadeva and his successor, were also buried near the eastern gate. As such, today, there are three Samadhs of the Mahants, within the Temple complex.

The second phase of desecration of the holiest Buddhist shrine by the Mahant began when he thought of converting the Great Temple as a Siva temple. That the Hindu Mahants, occupying the Maha Bodhi Temple, had nothing but hatred and scorn for the Buddha is evident from what Hamilton Buchanan, the first British to visit Buddha Gaya, saw in 1811. Buchanan records worship being offered to the Bodhi Tree by the Hindu pilgrims, but adds that "some zealous persons had lately built a stairway on the side of the terrace so that orthodox may pass without entering the porch and thus seeing the hateful image of the Buddha."

After the visit of Buchanan in 1811, the Mahant took another step to convert the Maha Bodhi Temple into a Hindu Temple. He dismantled the intervening wall, removed the Buddha statue, and established right in front of the throne a Siva-lingam. In this context, Rajendralal Mitra says:

> "In the 8th or 9th century, the last image (of the Buddha) was evidently lost, and in its place was set up a black stone image, which I believe was removed by one of the Mahants of the math when he consecrated a lingam in the middle of the sanctuary. . . . The lingam established in the centre of the square area in front of the throne is not an ordinary figure of the kind, but a big votive stupa, which has been made to do duty for it. It is still worshipped by the Mahant of the Math." (83-84, Buddha Gaya.)

Yet another addition made by the Mahant in the Temple complex is the so-called Panch Pandava temple which is just in front of the eastern gate of the Maha Bodhi Temple. In one of the rooms of this shabby structure built by the Mahant, there are five images of the Buddha in meditation. There is also a standing image of Maha Maya, the mother of Buddha. However, these are described as the images of the five Pandava brothers, and of Draupadi. To conceal their identity, they are covered with clothes.

Besides these additions and alterations in the Temple complex, the Mahant also destroyed and desecrated at will the Buddhist sculptures, and used them as building material. The Mahant even refused to part with them when the British Government asked for some of them for being restored in the Temple complex again. According to Sir Edwin Arnold, the celebrated author of The Light of Asia:

> "So strong have they (Mahants) become in ownership, that when the Bengal Government was in 1880 repairing the temple and its grounds, and begged for its embellishment from the Mahant a portion of Asoka's stone railing which he had built into his own house, the old Brahman would not give it up, and Sir Ashley Eden could not, or did not, compel the restoration."

What Edwin Arnold saw during his visit to Buddha Gaya in 1885 brought tears into his eyes. He later wrote:

> "When I sojourned in Buddha Gaya a few year ago, I was grieved to see Maharatta peasants performing "Shraddh" in such a place, and thousands of precious ancient relics of carved stone inscribed with Sanskrit lying in piles around. I asked the priest if I might have a leaf from the sacred tree.
>
> "Pluck as many as ever you like, sahib," was his reply, "it is nought to us."
>
> Ashamed of his indifference, I took silently the three or four dark shining leaves which he pulled from the bough over his head, and carried them with me to Ceylon. There I found them prized by the Sinhalese Buddhists with eager and passionate emotions."

Sir Edwin Arnold further says:

> "If you walked in that spot which all these scores of millions of our race love so dearly, you would observe with shame and grief in the mango groves, to the east of Lilajan, ancient statues plastered to the walls of an irrigating well near the village Mucharin identified with the "Muchalinda" tank. Stone carved with Buddha's images are to be found used as weights to the leavers for drawing water. I have seen ryots in the villages surrounding the temple using beautifully carved blocks as steps to their huts. I have seen three feet high statues in an excellent state of preservation, buried under rubbish to the east of the Mahant's baradari. A few are plastered into the eastern outer wall of the garden along the bank of Lilajan; and the Asoka pillars, the most ancient relics of the site—indeed "the most

antique memorials of all India," — which graced the temple pavement, are now used as posts of the Mahant's kitchen."

This was in 1885, and a century later the position was no better. Rather it was worse as I discovered during my second visit to Buddha Gaya in April 1979 when I made a thorough study of the Temple complex and all the other sites associated with the Buddha. At Bakraur, where Sujata Kutir is located, we found a number of fine Buddha images being spoiled by oil and colour etc., by the priest of the Shiva Temple which now stands on the site. On our way back from Bakraur, we came through the main gate of the Mahant's Math, the gate which opens on the river side. We (my wife and I) were shocked when our guide showed us the ancient sculptures having small Buddha images used in the very first step of the gate, the gate through which day in and day out, the Mahant and his men pass trampling these Buddha images under their feet.

Distressed by what I saw at Buddha Gaya during this visit, I wrote to the Director General, Archaeological Survey of India on 27 April 1979 requesting him to take remedial action so as to stop forthwith the shameful sacrilege of the Buddhist images by the Mahant. I also requested in my letter that the Buddha images kept in the courtyard of the Shiva Temple in the Mahant's Math be acquired by the ASI, and preserved in the Archaeological Museum at Buddha Gaya. On 1 June 1979, I was informed by the Archaeological Survey of India, New Delhi that "the matter is being looked into." My letter, and ASI's interim reply thereto are reproduced below to make the position clear:

D.C. Ahir A-2/30 Janakpuri

Deputy Secretary to the Govt. of India NEW DELHI — 110058.

Date : 24th April '79

To

The Director General,

Archeological Survey of India,

New Delhi.

Sir,

This is just to bring to your kind notice that there are a number of fine specimen of the Buddha images in the custody of the Mahant at Buddha Gaya and other Hindu priests such as incharge of the Shiva Temple at Bakraur. Not only that, during my recent visit to Buddha Gaya I found that Buddha images are still being desecrated at these places. In the main shrine and all around the Hindu Shiva Temple which now stands on the spot where Sujata offered food to the Buddha, there are fine images of the Buddha which are being spoiled by oil and colour etc. Behind this temple is the spot where the Buddha was actually sitting at the time Sujata offered food. Ancient stupas are still visible there but no steps have been taken to protect the same.

2. The most shocking thing is the continuous sacrilege and desecration of the Buddha images by the Mahant. On our way back from Bakraur, we came through the main gate of the Mahant's Math. We were shocked to see the ancient sculptures having small Buddha images used in the very first step of the gate. Day in and day out, the Mahant and his men pass through this gate trampling Buddha images under their feet. The Shiva temple in the Math has in its courtyard a large number of beautiful Buddha images in various postures. They are not worshipped but are used as decoration.

3. It is rather surprising that the Buddhist objects at these places have not been so far acquired by the Archaeological Department. The result is that the Archaeological Museum at Buddha Gaya is a museum in name only. Even though the great Mahabodhi Temple had a chequered history from 2nd Century AD to 12th Century AD yet the museum has no objects from the period from 2nd Century AD to 8th Century AD. The finest specimen of Buddha images/sculptures of this period are in the custody of the Mahant and other Hindu priests at Bakraur etc.

4. In order to stop sacrilege and desecration of Buddha images and to preserve the ancient Buddha images, it is requested that immediate steps may kindly be taken as indicated below:—

(a) the panel of Buddha images used in the steps of the main gate of the Mahant's Math should be removed and placed in the Archaeological Museum;
(b) all the Buddha images in the Math premises and at Bakraur should be removed to the Archaeological Museum; and
(c) the spot where Sujata offered food to the Buddha should be marked and protected.

5. Action taken in the matter may kindly be intimated in due course.

Thanking you in anticipation,

Yours faithfully,

(D.C. Ahir)

Copy forwarded for information
to the Curator, Archaeological Museum,
Buddha Gaya, Bihar.
Copy also forwarded for information to:

1. Venerable Gyan Jagat, Superintendent, The Mahabodhi Temple Management Committee, Buddha Gaya, Bihar.
2. Venerable Pannarama, Mahabodhi Society of India, Buddha Gaya, Bihar.

(D.C. Ahir)

No. 24/46/79-M

Government of India
Archaeological Survey of India

New Delhi, the 30th May, 1979.
1 JUN 1979

To

Shri D.C. Ahir,
Deputy Secretary to the Government of India,
A-2/30, Janak Puri,
New Delhi — 110058.

Sub: Preservation of Buddhist images kept under custody of the Mahants and Priests at Buddha Gaya and Bakraur by removing them in the Archaeological Museums.

Sir,

I am directed to refer to your letter dated 24.4.79 on the subject cited above and to inform you that the matter if being looked into.

Yours faithfully,

(K.V. Soundara Rajan)
Director (Monuments)
for Director-General

Thereafter, I also reminded personally the concerned official but in vain. Hence, I again wrote to the ASI on 24 November 1981 vide my letter reproduced below:

> "I am to invite your attention to your letter No. 24/46/79-M dated the 1 June, 1979 on the subject noted above and to request that the action taken in the matter may kindly be intimated as early as possible.
>
> 2. In the light of the recent theft of valuable Buddha images from the Archaeological Museum of Buddha Gaya, preservation of Buddhist images kept under custody of the Mahants and Priests etc. has become more urgent. I hope you will kindly look into the matter and do the needful."

Even then there was no response, no action, and the matter rested there. In the meanwhile, I again visited Buddha Gaya in April 1982, and requested Ven. Gyan Jagat, Superintendent of the Buddha Gaya Management Committee to pursue the matter with the Mahant but he expressed his inability to do so. Hence, sacrilege of the Buddha images by the Mahant and his men continued unchecked.

In December 1990, I once again visited Buddha Gaya, and with the help of a guide, I went inside the Mahant's math to check up the position. On reaching the outer gate, opening on the river side, I was happy to find that the Buddha images had been removed from the steps of the gate. On enquiry, I was told by the guide that the said images had not been removed by the Mahant or by any official agency but the same had been stolen by the thieves a few months back. This is how the most shameful sacrilege of the Buddha images by the Mahant and his men came to an end.

As for the Buddha images and other sculptures kept in the courtyard of the Shiva Temple in the Mahant's compound, these are still there. But how long they will be safe it is difficult to say. The collection of stone images in the Mahant's compound includes the following important images: 1. Standing Buddha, 5th century, 1.6 metres 2. Seated Buddha sheltered by Muchalinda, 8th century, 67 m. 3. Tara, 9th century, 1.51 m., and 4. Trailokvijaya, 10th century, 1.9 m. One fails to understand why they cannot be acquired by the Archaeological Survey of India, and preserved in the Buddha Gaya Site Museum, which in any case has very few good exhibits at present.

The Great Maha Bodhi Temple remained under the control of the Mahant till 1953 when the first Joint Hindu-Buddhist Management

Committee was constituted by the Government of Bihar under the Bodh Gaya Temple Act, 1949. The story of the epic struggle by the Buddhists to have the Maha Bodhi Temple liberated from the clutches of the Mahant will be told in a subsequent chapter.

Chapter X

BURMA'S ANOTHER EFFORT TO REPAIR THE TEMPLE

After the visit of the royal mission sent to Buddha Gaya in the fifteenth century, there was practically no contract between Burma and the Buddha's Seat of Enlightenment for nearly 400 years. The primary reason for this being the political upheaval in Burma after the fall of the Pagan kingdom in the thirteenth century as a result of the Tartar invasions. Then for a while Burmese power and political unity was restored in the sixteenth century but it was again disturbed in the eighteenth century by constant raids from across the borders. The crisis reached its peak when in 1752 the Talaings sacked the Burmese capital, Ava, and burnt it.

At such a critical juncture, an obscure village headman, A-Laung-Pa-Ya, who claimed descent from the Royal house of Pagan, appeared on the scene, and showed great courage in ending the chaos. He organised the local populace, and challenged the invaders. His victories were swift and decisive. In 1753, he occupied Ava, and declared himself the king. In 1755, he conquered Prome. And in 1756, he occupied the village where stood the great Shwe Dagon Pagoda, and gave the place a new name — Yankon (yan, victory; kon, accomplished) which later came to be known as Rangoon. Though A-Laung-Pa-Ya lived only for seven years after founding the kingdom, yet he left behind a strong and powerful ruling house.

After A-Laung-Pa-Ya's death in 1760, three kings ruled for a short period of 22 years. Then came his youngest son, Ba-Daw-Pa-Ya, who ruled successfully for a long period of 37 years from 1782 to 1819. It was during his reign that the Burmese contact with Buddha Gaya was revived again. He sent a royal mission in 1810 which carried out some minor repairs to the Maha Bodhi Temple. Next year, in 1811, the king himself came on a pilgrimage to Buddha Gaya.

Another Burmese mission came in 1823, with offerings for the Great Temple, which were sent by Ba-Gyi-Daw, who ascended the throne in 1819 and ruled till 1837.

The last effort by Burma to repair and restore the decaying Maha Bodhi Temple was made by King Mindon Min, who ruled the Kingdom of Pagan majestically for 25 years from 1853 to 1878. King Mindon was a very devout Buddhist. He is better known as the builder of Mandalay, his new capital, and the convenor of the Fifth Buddhist Council in Burma. The Fifth Council held at Mandalay under the patronage of the king Mindon-Min in 1871 was attended by 2400 distinguished monks and Dhamma teachers. The recitation, comparison and collation of the Pali Tripitaka continued for five months under the guidance of eminent Maha Theras. Thereafter, the entire Tripitaka was recorded on 729 marble slabs selected for the purpose.

On coming to know that the holy shrine at Buddha Gaya with which Burma had long association, was in a very bad shape, almost falling, King Mindon-Min decided to carry out extensive repairs to the Maha Bodhi Temple. Accordingly, in 1874, the King of Burma sent an embassy to the Government of India, with costly gifts for the Bodhi Tree and the Temple requesting the Government of India to extend all possible assistance to the mission to offer worship at the holy Bodhi Tree and the sacred Temple on his behalf.

The Government of India passed on this request of the Burmese King to the District Magistrate of Gaya for ascertaining the views of the Mahant who had claimed the Temple and the land around it as his own property. Consequently, the District Magistrate, Mr. Palmer, wrote a letter to the Mahant seeking his approval to the proposals of the King of Burma. His letter, inter-alia, noted:

> "The King of Burma desires that the compound of the Bodhi Tree which may have decayed on account of age be repaired. It is also his wish that two persons be deputed near the Bodhi Tree. He also wishes that once or twice a year, his people may make offerings to the Bodhi Tree as they may desire."

In response to this letter, the Mahant replied: As to the compound of the tree which the King of Burma wishes to repair, his Majesty is at liberty to do so if he so desires. The King of Burma may at his pleasure depute persons to officiate at the worship of the said Bodhi Tree.''

On receipt of this reply from the Mahant, through the District Magistrate of Gaya, the royal mission sent by the king Mindon-Min of Burma made the offerings at the Temple. The offerings consisted of 511 diamonds, 311 emeralds, 3966 rubies and 623 pearls together many ornaments from the Royal Relatives, Ministers and populace. A Pali inscription giving details of the offerings as well as the deeds done by King Mindon-Min, discovered at Buddha Gaya, reads as follows:

''King Mindon-Min, who founded the town of Mandalay, was the foremost among kings and monarchs and was the possessor of immense wealth, elephants and horses. He ruled the people with righteousness giving them just laws following the example of King Siri Dhammasoka and other powerful kings and was thus a descendant of the rulers of the world. Being inclined towards religious practices leading to the attainment of Arhatship, he was closely related to those Arhats and gives encouragement towards the attainment of NIRVANA, a cessation of the troubles and miseries of the three worlds. He carried out several meritorious deeds unceasingly, and among others these may be mentioned: Being a devout follower of Buddha, he took the most active part towards the propagation of Buddha's Sasana, and kept a strict watch over it, weeding out all that was bad. These words are true. This King, named Siri Pawara Vijayanantaya Sapandita Tatraditrapadi Maha Dhamma Rajadi Raja became the most powerful and famous King in the year 2396 of Buddha's Sasana and 1214th year of the Burmese era on a Thursday, the 11th day of the waxing of the month of Taboung. He was crowned King together with the Queen. Being a devout follower of Buddha, he made a determination that he would become an heir to all the riches of Buddha's Sasana and act as a guardian over it just as Buddha once said that his Sasana would be maintained by just and noble minded persons long after his Nirvana. King Mindon-Min then erected the Maha Loka Marazain Pagoda at Mandalay and also stone inscriptions of the whole of the three Pitakas. He further encouraged Bhikkhus to learn the Pitakas word for word and held the 5th Great Council. Not contended with these only, the King had a great desire to propagate Buddha's Sasana in other countries out of Burma, especially in Majihima Desa, where the Sasana had once flourished, but had almost died out.

He made arrangements to send Bhikkhus on mission to Majhima Desa to spread Buddha's Sasana, to make offerings at the Maha Bodhi Shrine, the most sacred spot on the surface of the earth where Lord Buddha had attained Omniscience and become Enlightened. He also had a desire to send out missions to other countries. Then in the month of Tasoungamon in the year 1236 of the Burmese era, in 2417th year of Buddha's Sasana, King Mindon-Min sent Minister Siri Maha Sayathu, Secretary Mindon Sithu and Corresponding Secretary Mindon Kyaw going together with followers on a pilgrimage to Maha Bodhi to make these offerings consisting of 511 diamonds, 311 emeralds, 3966 rubies and 623 pearls together with many ornaments from the Royal Relatives, Ministers and populace. With these offerings, the pilgrimage started on its journey on board the steamer 'Sakkya Yinmoon.' King Mindon-Min then prayed that by virtue of these meritorious deeds, he might attain Arhatship and make a declaration that he shared his merits with all the people of the world and living beings. Thus this is a record on stone of all the deeds done by King Mindon-Min."

Having made over the costly offerings to the Mahant, the Burmese royal mission left for Burma to report to the pious king.

Subsequently, the Foreign Minister of the Government of Burma wrote to the Agent of the Governor General on 18 August 1875 as follows:

"The locality where stands the Mahabodhi tree of India being the original spot where the Omniscient and Most Excellent Lord, on His blossoming to the dignity of Buddhahood, understood the four great Truths, extraordinary reverence and honour should be paid to it. His Majesty the King accordingly desires to do that homage; 1. by repairing the Mahayan or sacred enclosure, now in a state of decay, of the Mahabodhi tree; 2. by the repair of the sacred chaitya built by the King Dharmasoka over the site of Aparajita Throne; 3. by firmly propping up with masonry the right branch of the Mahabodhi tree; 4. by repairing all ruined structures connected with the treasures situated within the enclosure of the Mahabodhi tree; 5. by building near the Mahabodhi tree a monastery capable of containing about 20 Royal Rahans who will live there continually to perform the Bodhiranjan duties, namely, those connected with lighting of lamps and those connected with the presentation of flowers and cold water; 6. by enclosing the above Royal Monastery with a solid wall of masonry; 7. by hiring men to live on the spot to watch and to attend to the wants of the monastery; 8. by erecting a paribhoga for the deposit of the Royal offerings to the Mahabodhi Tree. Orders have consequently been given to the Royal scribe at Calcutta to submit plans and estimates for the completion of the above mentioned items."

The Mahant conveyed his consent to all the proposals. His only condition was that the Brahmanical idols lying the in compound of the Maha Bodhi Temple should neither be destroyed not interferred with.

On completion of all such preliminaries, the Burmese delegation returned once again to Buddha Gaya, and the actual repairing and restoration work began in 1877. Unfortunately, however, as the work was just to pick up King Mindon-Min died in September 1878. His death greatly upset the schedule. Moreover, the task was stupendous and it required lot of planning, patience and perseverance coupled with expert knowledge of archaeology. Since the Burmese were inexperienced, they failed in their last effort to repair and renovate the Maha Bodhi Temple, the Temple to which they had been so much emotionally attached for nearly 1000 years. But their effort was not in vain. Their failure proved to be a blessing in disguise; it prompted the British Government of India to step in, and do something to save the historic Buddhist shrine.

Chapter XI

REPAIRS AND RESTORATION BY THE BRITISH

The romantic story of re-discovery of the Buddhist monuments in ruins or just forgotten, having been engulfed by thick jungle began in the eighteenth century when the British Civil Servants began to take interest in India's past. The first British Officer to visit Buddha Gaya was Hamilton Buchanan of Indian Medical Service. He was there in 1811, and what he saw saddened him a lot. The Maha Bodhi Temple was in utter ruins, and there were no Buddhists around to look after the shrine. Fifty years later, in 1861, Cunningham found the Mahant and his men indulging in all sorts of un-Buddhistic ceremonies in the main shrine. Further, the Mahant, after the visit of Buchanan in 1811, had removed the Buddha image, and installed a Sivalingam in the centre of the square area in front of the throne.

The advent of Sir Alexander Cunningham was a turning point in the history of Buddhism in India. Born in England in 1814, Cunningham came to India in 1833 as a second lieutenant. While in service, he distinguished himself as an able administrator, surveyor and engineer. He also developed a keen interest in archaeology in order to understand India's past, the past that was primarily Buddhist. It was Cunningham who opened the Great Stupas of Sanchi in 1851, and discovered the relics of Sariputta and Moggallana, the two chief disciples of the Buddha. Cunningham was undoubtedly the greatest archaeologist and hero of the renaissance period. Consequent upon his retirement from the Army in 1861, General Cunningham was appointed as the first Director General of the Archaeological Survey established by the Government of India. Cunningham's zeal and interest in the archaeological material opened a new vista in the study of Indian Archaeology. Notwithstanding the risks involved in travel in those days as roads were rough or non-existent, and banditry was widespread, Cunningham himself went round; visited all the ancient sites; and prepared a systematic geographical map of ancient India. In his monumental work "Ancient Geography of India, Part I, the Buddhist Period." Cunningham recapitulated the glorious history of the Buddhist remains and monuments scattered all over the country.

Alexander Cunningham was especially fascinated by the Great Maha Bodhi Temple at Buddha Gaya, the sole surviving symbol of the glorious epoch of Buddhism in India. Hence, he returned again and again to Buddha Gaya. During his second visit to Buddha Gaya in December 1862, Cunningham decided to carry out excavation in the vicinity of the Great Temple so as to find some evidence of its past history. However, this he could do only in 1871 when he made the most significant discovery of two gold impressions of a gold coin of Huvishka, the Kushana king who flourished in the second century AD, along with the relics, deposited under the inner throne in the main chamber, by the builders of the Temple in the second century AD. This discovery solved to a great extent the mystery of the period of construction of the Great Temple.

The present Bodhi Tree was also planted by the loving hands of Cunningham when the old Tree fell during a storm in 1876. Cunningham tells the story of the Bodhi Tree as follows:

> "In December 1862, I found this Tree 'very much decayed; one large stem to the westward, with three branches was still green, but the other branches were barkless and rotten.' I next saw the Tree in 1871, and again in 1875, when it had become completely decayed, and shortly afterwards in 1876, the only remaining portion of the Tree fell over the west wall during a storm, and the Old Pipal Tree was gone. Many seeds, however, had been collected, and young scions of the parent tree were already in existence to take its place." (Cunningham, Mahabodhi: p. 20.)

In 1876, in fact, two Bo-saplings were planted — one in its original place to the west of the Temple, and the other to the north thereof.

When the Burmese were struggling with the stupendous task of repairs to the Maha Bodhi Temple, a journalist from Calcutta visited Buddha Gaya in 1879 to see for himself the progress of repairs to the Temple being carried out by the Burmese. His report appeared in "Englishman," a paper published from Calcutta, and gave a graphic picture of the decaying Temple in these words:

"The whole of plinth and lower mouldings buried under accumulation of rubbish; the floor of the sanctum and of the great hall in front 4 feet lower than the level of rough stone floor laid by the Burmese, who had partially cleared away the rubbish in front; the great hall roofless; the half hall or porch of the second storey roofless; the whole of the front of the Temple above the third chamber fallen, disclosing a great triangular gap 20 feet high and 12 feet wide at base; the whole of the facade of the platform to the east a mound of ruins; the whole south facade of platform ruinous, but retaining here and there portions of original work; the entire west face of the Temple buried under rubbish." (Ibid. p. 3.)

This report of an independent correspondent opened the eyes of the Government of India, and recognising its archaeological and historical value, the Government decided to repair and restore the Temple itself. Accordingly Sir Ashley Eden, the Lt. Governor of Bengal appointed, in 1880, J.D. Belgar, one of Cunningham's assistants, to make a thorough repair of the Temple. The restoration and renovation of the Maha Bodhi Temple to its present condition almost an exact replica of the original shrine, was a lengthy affair and cost a great deal of money but was accomplished with rare devotion and dedication by Beglar. He restored it on the basis of a small model in stone of the Temple found amongst the ruins near the Temple. Based on this model, Beglar also restored the front pavilion and the four corner towers. For this addition, Beglar was criticised by many persons. However, Cunningham justified it by saying:

"This additional work has been much criticised, and I have been roundly abused for it in company with Beglar, although I had nothing whatever to say to it. At the same time I must confess that, since I have seen it, I think his design of the front Pavilion is a very successful completion of the entrance in the style and spirit of the original work as shown in the model. It is of course a *restoration,* which, as it was based on the double authority of existing remains and an ancient model. I consider legitimate and justifiable."

(Ibid. Preface, p. i.)

The restoration of the Maha Bodhi Temple was done by Beglar in good faith and to the best of his ability. The Buddhists ought to be grateful to him, and the then British Government of India which met the entire expenditure of over rupees one lakh incurred on the restoration work. As for the four corner towers, Beglar seems to have done the right thing in adding these towers. As says Ven. S. Dhammika:

"Although these additions in their present form may not correspond exactly to how the temple looked in the medieval period, few can doubt that Beglar's restoration gave the temple back its majesty. Beglar understood that the Mahabodhi Temple was never meant to be a dead relic for students of archaeology and architecture to study, but celebration in brick and stone of the Buddha's enlightenment and a proper temple where Buddhists could come and worship."

(Middle Land Middle Way: p. 62.)

The Great Maha Bodhi Temple, as restored in the 1880's is in essence the same building that was seen by Hiuen Tsang in 637 AD. According to Cunningham:

"This description of the Mahabodhi Temple, as it stood in AD 637, tallied so closely with the Great Temple as it now stands, that, in my opinion, there can be no reasonable doubt that it is, in spite of all its repairs and alterations, the same building which was described by the Chinese pilgrim, as will be seen by the following comparison.

1st The dimensions of the two Temples are exactly the same, the present building being 48 feet square at its base, and between 160 and 170 feet in height. In 1861 my measurement of its height, in its broken state, was 160 feet from the floor of the chamber to the top of the ruined pinnacle. It is now, after repair of the pinnacle, upwards of 170 feet.

2nd It is built of bluish bricks, with a coating of plaster.

3rd The four faces present several tiers of niches, rising one above the other, each of which, no doubt, one held a Buddhist figure. Only three figures remained when I first saw the building.

4th The entrance on the eastern side was certainly an addition to the original building, as its courses of bricks did not correspond with those of the main body of the Temple."

(Cunningham, Mahabodhi: p. 18.)

Having restored the Great Temple to its original majestic look, Beglar found that the god of the shrine, the original image of the Blessed One was missing from the sanctum. The reason being that the Buddha image had been removed by the Mahant some time during the first half of the nineteenth century so as to convert it into a Siva temple. The story of the Buddha images enshrined from time to time in the Great Temple is told by Rajendralal Mitra in these words:

> "On this throne there was originally an image of the Buddha in gold, but in the fifth or sixth century it was replaced by a black basalt one, which was seen by the Chinese pilgrim in the seventh century.
>
> In the eighth or ninth century the last image was evidently lost, and in its place was set up black stone image which I believe was removed by one of the Mahant of the Math when he consecrated a lingam in the middle of the sanctuary." (R.L. Mitra, Buddha Gaya: pp. 83-84.)

The great gilded image of the Blessed One in the earth-touching attitude (bhumisparsa mudra), dating from the tenth century AD, that had been uprooted by the Mahant, after the visit of Buchanan in 1811, was brought back by Cunningham and Beglar and re-enshrined in its original place, the main chamber of the Maha Bodhi Temple. It is the largest seated image of the Buddha found at Buddha Gaya. It shows the Buddha sitting on a patterned cushion instead of lotus; the earth goddess appears in the middle of the pedestal which is also ornamented with lions alternating with elephants. An effaced inscription on the edge of the pedestal noted by R.L. Mitra and Cunningham gives the Buddhist creed and the name of the donor Purnabhadra.

According to Cunningham:

> "The largest figure of Buddha now existing is that which has recently been enshrined inside the Great Temple. It was formerly hidden inside a small room in the courtyard of the Brahmanical monastery, but it was given up by the Mahant to replace the brick and mud modern statue set up by the Burmese. The figure is $5\frac{1}{2}$ feet in height, which is far below the dimensions of the old statue seen by Hwen Thang, who records that it was 11 feet 5 inches in height, with a breadth across the shoulders of 6 feet 2 inches, and across the knees of 8 feet 8 inches." (Mahabodhi: pp. 64-65.)

As a natural consequence of having repaired and resotred the Great Maha Bodhi Temple at an enormous cost, the Government of India also took over the responsibility of upkeep and maintenance of the Temple in future, and placed the building under the supervision of a government official. In an order dated the 25 July 1889, George A. Grierson, District Magistrate of Gaya, noted:

> "Mr Maddox is placed incharge of Bodh Gaya Temple and Bungalow. He should visit it once a month and see that the drains are kept clear and that the other things insisted upon by me are carried out. He should also see that the Bungalow is kept in watertight repair, and that the chaityas and other stone-relics are not carried away." (R.B. Lal, Bodh Gaya — Past and Present: p. 14.)

In pursuance of this order, the Maha Bodhi Temple was taken over by the Public Works Department, Bihar in 1890 for maintenance purposes. Thus, the Great Temple came under dual control of the Government and the Mahant. While the property rights remained with the Mahant, the upkeep of the Temple was taken over by the Government of Bihar, and it remained so till the Buddha Gaya Temple Management Committee was constituted in 1953.

Chapter XII

SIR EDWIN ARNOLD PLEADS THE BUDDHIST CASE

The first person to raise the question of the restoration of the Buddha Gaya Temple to the Buddhists, its rightful owners, was Sir Edwin Arnold, the celebrated author of 'The Light of Asia,' the epic poem on the life of the Buddha. Born on 10 July 1832 at Gravesend, Kent, England, Edwin Arnold came to India in November 1857, consequent upon his appointment as Principal of Deccan College, Poona. Though he was in India only for four years yet during this short period he had developed a keen interest in Buddhism. In 1861, Arnold returned to London where he got a job as a feature writer with the Daily Telegraph, a paper of which he later became Editor. Meanwhile, he continued his study of Buddhism on the basis of whatever literature on Buddhism was available in those days. In 1879, he published his famous poem, The Light of Asia, which became an instant success. In his Preface to this book, Arnold wrote:

> "A generation ago little or nothing was known in Europe of this great faith of India which had nevertheless existed during twenty-four centuries, and at this day surpasses, in the number of its followers and the area of its prevalence, any other form of creed, Four hundred and seventy millions of our race live and die in the tenets of Gautama; and the spiritual dominions of this ancient teacher extend at the present time, from Nepal and Ceylon, over the whole Eastern Peninsula, to China, Japan, Tibet, Central Asia, Siberia, and even Swedish Lapland. India itself might fairly be included in this magnificent Empire of Belief; for though the profession of Buddhism has for the most part passed away from the land of its birth, the mark of Gautama's sublime teaching is stamped ineffaceably upon modern Brahmanism, and the most characteristic habits and convictions of the Hindus are clearly due to the benign

influence of Buddha's precepts. More than one third of mankind, therefore, owe their moral and religious ideas to this illustrious prince, whose personality, though imperfectly revealed in the existing sources of information, cannot but appear the highest, gentlest, holiest, and most beneficent."

In 1885, Sir Edwin Arnold visited Buddha Gaya, and paid his homage in person to the Great Buddha in the Maha Bodhi Temple which had just been repaired and restored by the British Government of India. He was thrilled to see the Great Temple but was also grieved to find the holy place still being desecrated by the Saivite Mahant. When Edwin Arnold asked the Mahant, whether he could take a few green leaves of the Bodhi Tree, "Pluck as many you like, sahib; it is naught to us," said the Hindu priest. Arnold silently took three or four leaves from the bough over his head.

From India, Edwin Arnold crossed over to Sri Lanka. Wherever he went in that Buddhist land, he received a rousing reception. At Kandy, where stands the Temple of Tooth of Buddha, Arnold was overwhelmed when the Bodhi-leaf, which he had brought from Buddha Gaya, presented to the monks there, was not only received with "eager and passionate emotion," but was placed in a casket of gold, and made the centre of weekly pooja. No wonder, when the people of Sri Lanka begged Arnold to plead their case, before the appropriate Governmental authorities in India and U.K., that the Buddha Gaya Temple be handed over to the Buddhists, he readily agreed to do so.

Soon after his return to London, Sir Edwin Arnold took up the matter with all the concerned highest authorities in India and U.K. and pleaded with them that the holy Buddhist shrine at Buddha Gaya be made over to its rightful owners, the Buddhists, if necessary, after paying suitable compensation to the Hindu Mahant. He put the compensation at Rupees one lakh, which he thought the Government of India could bear, and failing that he promised to raise the required amount from the Buddhist countries to acquire the Temple. He kept up the crusade, almost single-handed, for the next 5-6 years and wrote a series of articles in the Daily Telegraph which created a stir in the Buddhist world.

In 1893, Edwin Arnold published an article in the Daily Telegraph under the title "East and West: A Splendid Opportunity" and made a forceful plea to the British Government to acquire the Maha Bodhi Temple and hand it over to the Buddhists, its rightful owners. But his appeal fell on deaf ears. Neither the Government of India nor the

Government of U.K. showed any keenness to pursue the suggestion. In the meanwhile, in the context of Anagarika Dharmapala's movement for regaining the control of the Maha Bodhi Temple, there was a sudden change in the attitude of the Mahant from meek 'co-operation' to open 'confrontation.'' As a result, the Government panicked, and to keep peace, cold-shouldered Arnold's suggestion. Thus a splendid opportunity was lost by the Government of India, and the Buddhists had to srruggle hard for nearly 60 years to oust the Mahant.

Since the powerful article describes vividly what Edwin Arnold saw at Buddha Gaya in 1885, and what efforts he made to secure the Great Temple for the Buddhists, a slightly abridged version of this inspiring article is appended here:

EAST AND WEST — A SPLENDID OPPORTUNITY

by

SIR EDWIN ARNOLD,
M.A., KC.I.E., C.S.I.

I would today, in these columns (*Daily Telegraph*), respectfully invite the vast and intelligent British public to forget, for a little while, home weather and home politics, and to accompany me, in fancy, to a sunny corner of their empire, where there centres a far more important question, for the future of religion and civilisation, than any relating to parish councils or parish pumps. I will, by their leave, tell them of beautiful scenes under warm skies; of a temple fairer and more stately, as well as more ancient, than almost any existing fane; and will also show them how the Indian Government of Her Majesty, supported by their own enlightened opinion, might, through an easy and blameless act of administrative sympathy, render four hundred millions of Asiatics for ever the friends and grateful admirers of England.

We will spread the magic carpet of Kamar-az-zaman, told of in the ''*Arabian Nights*'' and pass at once upon it to Patna, the busy city beside the Ganges, some 350 miles by rail from Calcutta. The closing days of March are hot there, and the river glitters as if it were molten gold under the fiery sun. We will not stay accordingly to inspect the indigo factories; or to visit the wonderful Golah, where 140,000 tons of rice can be laid up; nor the government opium factory where enough of that most useful and benign drug is stored to put the whole world to sleep. We will take train from Bankipore for Gaya, only fifty-seven miles away, and having rested in that town for the night, we shall have ordered carriages to be ready at break of day to convey us four koss further—some seven or eight miles—into the hills which hereabout just across the valley of the Ganges.

I said you should see beautiful scenery, and surely this is such. The road, broad and well made, runs between the Gaya Hills on the right and the bright slow-stealing stream of the ancient Nilajan on the left. The mountain flanks are covered with cactus, wild indigo, and korinda bushes, showing a little temple perched upon almost every peak; while down on the flat, and especially along the sandy levels bordering the river, green stretches of palmgroves are interspersed with sal and tamarind trees, the undergrowth being long tigergrass and the common but ever-lovely ground palmetto, chamoerops humilis. The air, deliciously cool before the sun rises, is full of birds abroad for food — crows, parrakeets, mynas, the blue-winged rollers, the green and scarlet "hammer-smiths," black and white kingfishers, bee birds, bronze and emerald, with graceful silvery egrets stalking among the cattle. Later on, when the sky grows warmer, you will see clouds of lovely butterflies among the flowers of the orchids and poisonous datura, with sun-birds and dragonflies skimming along the blue and pink lotuses in the pools. The people whom we meet upon the road are dark-skinned patient peasants going with their products to Gaya and Bankipur, while those whom we shall overtake will be mainly pilgrims of the day wending their way to the immeasurably holy place towards which we also are bound. For, see! they also at the fifty mile quit the main track, and turning to the left by a less excellent but still carriageable road, which winds under the now welcome shade of the jak-trees and mangoes, are making for that most sacred spot of all hallowed places in Asia, towards which our own feet and thoughts are bound.

It is here! Beyond the little village of mud huts and the open space where dogs and children and cattle bask together in the dust, beyond the Mahunt's College, and yonder great fig tree which has split with its roots that wall, twelve feet thick, built before England had ever been discovered, nestles an abrupt hollow in the surface, symmetrical and well-kept, and full of stone images, terraces, balustrades, and shrines. It is oblong — as big, perhaps, altogether as Russell Square, and surrounded on its edges by small houses and buildings. From one extremity of the hallowed area rises with great beauty and majesty a temple of very special style and design. The plinth of the temple is square, with a projecting porch, and on the top of this soars to the sky a pyramidical tower of nine storeys, profusely embellished with niches, string courses, and mouldings, while from the truncated summit of this an upper pinnacle rears itself, of graceful form, topped by a gold finial, representing the amalaka fruit. A smaller pyramidical tower stands at each corner of the roof of the lower structure, and there is a broad walk round the base of the Great Tower. Over the richly worked porch which fronts the east a triangular aperture is pierced, whereby the morning glory of the sun may fall through upon the gilded image seated in the sanctuary within. That image, you will perceive, is — or was — of Buddha, and this temple is the holiest and most famous, as well as nearly the sole surviving shrine of all those eighty-four thousand fanes erected to the Great Teacher by King Asoka, two hundred and eighteen years after the Lord Buddha's Nirvana.

Yet more sacred even than the cool, dark sanctuary into which we look, to see the sunbeams kissing the mild countenance of the Golden Buddha inside; more intensely moving to the Buddhists who come hither, and richer with associations of unspeakable interest and honour than King Asoka's stately temple, or even those stone railings carved with mermaids, crocodiles, elephants, and lotus flowers, which the king himself commanded, and which still surround the shrine, is yonder square platform of stone, about a yard high from the ground, out of which a tree is growing. That is the Maha Bodhi tree — in the opinion of superstitious votaries the very original Bodhi tree, miraculously preserved— but more rationally that which replaces and represents the ever memorable shade under which the inspired Siddhartha state at the moment when he attained Sambodhi, the supreme light of his gentle wisdom. It is a fig tree — of the ficus Indica species — with the well known long glossy leaves. Its stem is covered with patches of gold leaf, and its boughs are hung with streamers of white and coloured cloth, while at its root — frequently watered by the pious with sandal oil and attar of roses — will probably be seen sitting a Brahman priest of the Saivite sect intoning mantras. You will hear him say, "Gaya! Gaya Sirsa, Bodhi Gaya," for though he is praying on behalf of Mahratta pilgrims, and does not know or care for Buddha, yet ancient formulas cling to the spot and to his lips. And, beyond all doubt, this is the spot most dear and divine, and precious beyond every other place on earth, to all the four hundred million Buddhists in China, Japan, Mongolia, Assam, Cambodia, Siam, Burma, Arakan, Nepaul, Thibet and Ceylon. This is the authentic site, and this the successor-tree, *by many unbrokenly cherished generations of that about which my "Light of Asia"* says:

"Then he arose, made strong by the pure meal,
And bent his footsteps where a great Tree grew,
The Bodhi tree (thenceforward in all years
Never to fade. and ever to be kept
In homage of the world, beneath whose leaves
It was ordained the Truth should come to Buddha,
Which now the Master knew; wherefore he went
With measured pace, steadfast, majestical,
Unto the Tree of Wisdom. Oh, ye worlds
Rejoice! Our Lord wended unto the Tree!"

There is no doubt, in fact, of the authenticity of the spot. The four most sacred places of Buddhism are Kapilavastu (now Bhuila), where Prince Siddhartha was born; Isipatana, outside Benares, where he first preached; Kusinara where he died; and this site marked by the tree, whereat "in the full moon of Wesak" 2483 years ago he mentally elaborated the gentle and lofty faith with which he has civilised Asia. And of all those four, the Tree-Place here at Buddha Gaya is the most dear and sacred to Asiatic Buddhists. Why, then, is it today in the hands of Brahman priest, who do not care about the temple, except for the credit of owning it, and for the fees which they draw? The facts are these. Until the thirteenth century — that is, for more than 1400 years — it was exclusively used and guardianed by Buddhists, but fell into decay and neglect, like other Buddhist temples, on the expulsion of Buddhism from India. Three hundred years ago a wandering Saivite ascetic visited the spot, and settled down, drawing round him gradually the beginning of what is now the College of Priests established there. So strong have they since become in ownership, that when the Bengal Government in 1880 was repairing the temple and its grounds, and begged for its embellishment from the Mahant a portion of Asoka's stone railing which he had built into his own house, the old Brahman would not give it up, and Sir Ashley Eden could not, or did not, compel the restoration.

The Buddhist world had indeed, well-nigh forgotten this hallowed and most interesting centre of their faith — the Mecca, the Jerusalem, of a million Oriental congregations — when I sojourned in Buddha Gaya a few years ago, I was grieved to see Maharatta peasants performing "Shraddh" in such a place, and thousands of precious ancient relics of carved stone inscribed with Sanskrit lying in piles around. I asked the priest if I might have a leaf from the sacred tree.

"Pluck as many as ever you like, sahib," was his reply, "it is nought to us."

Ashamed of his indifference, I took silently the three or four dark shining leaves which he pulled from the bough over his head, and carried them with me to Ceylon, having written upon each the holy Sanskrit formula. There I found them prized by the Sinhalese Buddhists with eager and passionate emotion. The leaf presented by me to the temple at Kandy, for example, was placed in a casket of precious metal and made the centre of a weekly service and there and then it befell that, talking to the gentle and learned priests at Panadure — particularly to my dear and wise friend, Sri Weligama — I gave utterance to the suggestion that the temple and its appurtenances ought to be, and might be by amicable arrangements with the Hindoo College and by the favour of the Queen's Government, placed in the hands of a representative committee of the Buddhist nations.

I think there never was an idea which took root and spread so far and fast as that thrown out thus to the sunny temple-court at Panadure, amid the waving taliputs. Like those tropical plants which can almost be seen to grow, the suggestion quickly became an universal aspiration, first in Ceylon and next in other Buddhist countries. I was entreated to lay the plan before the Oriental authorities, which I did. I wrote to Sir Arthur Gordon, Governor of Ceylon, in these words: "I suggest a Governmental Act, which would be historically just, which would win the love and gratitude of all Buddhist populations and would reflect enduring honour upon English administration. The temple and enclosure at Buddha-Gaya are, as you know, the most sacred spots in all the world for the Buddhists. But Buddha Gaya is occupied by a college of Saivite priests, who worship Mahadeva there, and deface the shrine with emblems and rituals foreign to its nature. That shrine and the ground surrounding it remain, however, government property, and there would be little difficulty, after proper and friendly negotiations, in procuring the departure of the Mahunt with his priests, and the transfer of the temple and its grounds to the guardianship of Buddhists from Ceylon and elsewhere. I have consulted high authorities, among them General Cunningham, who thoroughly sympathises with the idea, and declares it entirely feasible. . . . I apprehend that a certain sum of money might be required to facilitate the transfer of the Brahmans, and to establish the Buddhist College. In my opinion, a lakh of rupees could not be expended by any government in a more profitable manner.

Sir Arthur, who had just been exploring Buddhist remains in Ceylon, was very well disposed to the idea. Lord Dufferin warmly received it, at Calcutta; Lord Connemara, in Madras; and at that time, if only the Home-Government had been more alive to a grand opportunity, it would have been easy to make satisfactory terms with the Brahmans, and to have effected the transfer of the holy place to a representative committee — at one stroke delighting and conciliating all Buddhistic Asia.

But two or three years passed by, and while the idea was spreading throughout Asia, and a large society had become established with the special purpose of acquiring the guardianship of the sacred site, the Mahant grew more exacting in his expectations, and clung closer to the possession of the temple. The letters which I received from the East showed that the old Brahman had memorialized the government, in his alarm or avarice, and that local authorities had for quiet's sake reported adversely to the negotiation. I think the Mahant was a good man. I had never wished any but friendly and satisfactory arrangements with him. Yet you walked in that sopt which all these scores of millions of our race love so dearly, you would observe with shame and grief in the mango groves, to the east of Lilajan, ancient statues plastered to the walls of an irrigating well near the village Muchain—identified with the ''Machalinda'' tank. Stones carved with Buddha's images are to be found used as weights to the levers for drawing water. I have seen ryots in the villages surrounding the temple using beautifully-carved blocks as steps to their huts. I have seen three feet high statues in an excellent state of preservation, buried under rubbish to the east of the Mahant's baradari. A few are plastered into the eastern outer wall of the garden along the bank of Lilajan; and the Asoka pillars, the most ancient relics of the site — indeed ''the most antique memorials of all India,'' — which graced the temple pavement are now used as parts of the Mahant's kitchen.

To rectify this sad neglect, and to make the temple, what it should be, the living and learned centre of purified Buddhism, money was not, and is not, lacking. If the Home-Government had seen its way to make the Hindoo Abbot well-disposed. I could have commanded any sum which might have seemed fair and necessary. But the idea was too intelligent for the official grasp, and the golden moment went by.

Nevertheless, Asia did not abandon its new desire, and I received so many, and such pressing, communications, that I went at last to the then Indian Secretary of State, Lord Cross — always intelligent, kindly and receptive — and once more pleaded for the great restoration.

"Do you wish, Lord Cross," I asked, "to have four hundred millions of Eastern peoples blessing your name night and day, and to be for ever remembered in Asia, like Alexander or Asoka, or Akbar the Great?'

"God bless my soul, yes" answered the Minister; "how is that to be done?"

Then I repeated all the facts, and produced so happy an effect upon the Indian Minister's mind, that he promised to consult the Council, and to write — if the idea was approved — to Lord Landsdowne. In due time the Viceroy replied that the idea was legitimate and beneficial, and that so long as no religious ill-feeling was aroused, and no pecuniary grant asked from the Indian Treasury, the Calcutta Government would be inclined to favour any friendly negotiations. Thus the matter stood at my last visit to the east, when I was astonished and rejoiced to find how firmly the desire of this restoration had taken root, and how enkindled with the hope of it Ceylon, Siam, Burmah, and Japan had become. The Maha Bodhi Society, established to carry out the scheme, was constituted.

To give some faint idea of the interest felt in this matter even among such remote communities as those of Japan. I will speak of a scene in Tokyo still vivid in my memory. Last summer, in the Japanese capital, the Buddhist High Priest, with certain of the fraternity begged me to come to the temple in Atagoshita and speak to the brethren about the Holy Places in India, and especially upon the prospects of acquiring for the Buddhist world the guardianship of the Temple of the Tree. In the cool, dark inner court of that Japanese tera the priests and their friends sate on the white mats in concentric circles, eagerly listening while I told them all about that three or four hundred miles of Indian country lying between Busti in Oudh and Buddha Gaya in the Lower Provinces, which is the Holy Land of the "calm brethren of the yellow robe." I spoke of the birthplace and death-place of the Gentle Teacher, and showed them pictures which I had myself taken of the ancient building at Isipatana outside Benares. The hot day, beating upon the hillside beyond the temple garden, shone upon the scarlet azaleas and the lotus buds in the garden-lake, and rendered it warm enough, even in that vast shadowy apartment, for a constant flutter of fans, while now and then a young priest from the outer circle would glide away for drinking-water. Bu when I came to paint for them that site of the stately temple — which from its hollow beside Buddhist-tree, looks over the hill of the "Thousand Gardens," and marks the spot where the whole religious history of Asia was transformed, and its manners for ever stamped with the merciful tenderness and indestructible hopes of Buddhism — those hundreds of priests and novices sate like rows of little children lost in a fairy story. The fans were laid aside; the shaven heads were craned forward in intense desire to hear every word; old men laid their hands to their ears, and young ones leaned towards me with clasped palms, to learn all about the Tree, and the Temple, and the broken statues, and the Hindoo priests who do not care for the spirit of the place, and who ought, in a friendly way, to yield it up, on proper conditions, to Buddhist guardianship. Every man present would have given all he possessed. I think to hope towards such an end. As for their unworthy guest, they lavished upon me marks of pleasure and gratitude; they spread me out an outrageously elaborate feast table in the temple pavilion, and sent with me back to my lodgings servants carrying presents of books and boxes of beautiful Japanese silks and embroideries. Since then the High Priest writes to me thus from Tokyo:

"After your regretted departure from Japan the Indo-Busseki Kofuku Society has not been idle, and now I am glad to inform you that we are trying to buy a certain piece of land near each of the sacred sites according to your kind advice to us. Mr. Dharmapala, of the Maha Bodhi Society is doing all he can to help us in India; and if everything goes as intended, a certain number of Japanese monks will start for India within this year."

Thus is this new and great idea spreading, and the world will not be very much older, I think, before Buddhism by this gateway goes back to its own land, and India becomes the natural centre of Buddhistic Asia. For the moment I am sorry to say the movement has sustained a check. After a friendly correspondence in Sanskrit between the Mahant and myself, matters were looking fair for an arrangement, when — against my wish — hostile measures were commenced between the Maha Bodhi Society and the Hindoo monks. Mr. Dharmapala, the energetic secretary, whose enthusiastic services to the cause can never be sufficiently praised, and the example, of whose generous efforts ought to make him beloved throughout Buddhistic Asia — thought proper to place in the temple a very precious gilded image of Buddha, sent to his care from Japan. The Mahant's people ejected this, not without violence, and a series of lawsuits began. We gained the favourable decision of the resident official, and of the Suddar Court; but the High Court of Calcutta, by a judgment which I must respectfully declare erroneous and untenable, reversed the decree so that, after an expenditure of more than one hundred thousand rupees, and the bravest labours on the part of my excellent friend, Mr. Dharmapala, the policy of appealing to law has failed.

I am, however, quite certain that my own policy of appealing to Reason and Right, and of relying upon friendly negotiations with the present Hindoo tenants of the shrine, will and must eventually prevail. It is a fixed purpose of my mind that these shall prevail, and the first really enlightened Viceroy who takes up this question, will discern its huge political importance and assist me and my friends to obtain success. I suppose there are some people who will ask, why should the British public take any concern in such a movement? But such will be of much the same calibre as those who go about inquiring, "What is the British Empire to Battersea?" Apart from the immense historical, religious and social importance of Buddhism in Asia, here is an opportunity for the Government of India to gratify and conciliate half that continent by the easiest and least costly exercise of good-will. The Mahant and his college will, no doubt, have to be bought out and rather expensively, now that delays and misguided judgments have made him master of the bargaining. But if an enlightened Minister and Viceroy will, as they may, facilitate the arrangement, all must end well, and grateful Buddhists would furnish whatever cash is requisite. No orthodox Hindoos will be wounded in sentiment, because, by strict truth, the Mahant, as a Brahman and follower of Sankaracarya, goes against his shastras by keeping control of a Buddhists' temple. However, it brings him so much personal dignity and so much money, that these things must be compounded for, no doubt; yet a well-disposed, collected and a far-seeing government could find a score of pleasant ways to make him willing to give up his tenure. There is no room left me to dwell upon all the happy consequences which would flow to the Indian Viceroyalty and to India herself from the good-will so created in Burmah and Siam. Buddhism would return to the place of its birth, to elevate, to spiritualise, to help and enrich the population. It would be a new Asiatic crusade, triumphant without tears, or tyranny, or blood; and the Queen's administration would have the glory and benefit of it. The Hindu of Madras, a leading native journal, writes: "If there is anything in the intellectual and moral legacies of our forefathers of which we may feel proud, it is that sublime, pure and simple conception of a religious and moral system which the world owes to Buddha. Educated Hindoos cannot hesitate in helping Buddhism to find a commanding and permanent footing once more in their midst, and to live in mutually purifying amity with our Hinduism itself.'' Here is indeed, for an enlightened British Indian Minister, ''a splendid opportunity.''

Chapter XIII

ANAGARIKA DHARMAPALA'S EPIC STRUGGLE

Inspired by Sir Edwin Arnold's writings on Buddha Gaya, Anagarika Dharmapala, a young Sinhala Buddhist, who turned out to be the first great missionary of modern times, decided to see for himself the condition of Buddhist shrines in India. On 20 January 1891 Dharmapala, accompanied by — a Japanese monk, Kozen Gurаratana, visited Sarnath. He was shocked to see the horrible condition of the sacred site where Lord Buddha had preached His First Sermon and turned the Wheel of Dhamma. The holy Isipatana was completely in ruins, deserted, and haunt of the pigs. However, it was not at Sarnath, but at Buddha Gaya, which they reached on 22 January 1891, that Dharmapala was visibly moved on seeing the Maha Bodhi Temple being shamefully neglected and desecrated by the Hindu Mahant. Describing his experience, he wrote in his diary:

> "After driving 6 miles (from Gaya) we arrived at the holy spot. Within a mile you could see lying scattered here and there broken statues etc. of our blessed Lord. At the entrance to the Mahant's temple on both side's of the portico there are statues of our Lord in the attitude of meditation and expounding the Law. How elevating! The sacred Vihara — the Lord sitting on his throne and the great solemnity which pervades all round makes the heart of pious devotee weep. How delightful! As soon as I touched with my forehead the Vajrasana a sudden impulse came to my mind. It prompted me to stop here and take care of this sacred spot — so sacred that nothing in the world is equal to this place where Prince Sakya Sinha gained Enlightenment under the Bodhi Tree. . . . When the sudden impulse came to me I asked Kozen priest whether he would join me, and he joyously assented and more than this he had

been thinking the same thing. We both solemnly promised that we would stop here until some Buddhist priests came to take charge of the place."

Having resolved not to leave Buddha Gaya unless some arrangements had been made to look after the sacred shrine, Dharmapala moved to the nearby Burmese Rest House built in 1875 by King Mindon Min of Burma. As soon as he had settled there he started writing letters to scores of people in Sri Lanka, Burma and India describing the pitiable condition of the holiest of the holy Buddhist shrine, and pleading for their co-operation, help and assistance for the re-establishment of the Sangha there. In the meanwhile Dharmapala also made enquiries from the officials about the ownership of the Temple. When the Collector of Gaya, informed him that the Temple together with its revenues, belonged to the Mahant, adding that with the help of the Government it might be possible for the Buddhists to buy it from him, Dharmapala immediately started planning collection of the required funds, and left for Burma via Calcutta. After arousing interest of the Burmese Buddhists in the restoration of the Maha Bodhi Temple and having received promises for financial assistance, Dharmapala returned to Colombo in May 1891. And on May 31 there, he founded the 'The Buddha Gaya Maha Bodhi Society'; with himself as General Secretary, and Ven. Hikkaduwa Siri Sumangala Maha Nayaka Thera, Principal of the Vidyodaya Pirivena, Colombo, as President of the Society.

The purpose of the Society was thus stated:

"The site where the Divine Teacher attained supreme wisdom, now known as Buddha Gaya, is in middle India, and to his followers there is no spot on earth more sacred than the Bodhimanda, whereon stands the Bodhi Tree

"Never to fade, and ever to be kept
In homage of the world, beneath whose leaves
It was ordained the truth should come to Buddha.

"At this hallowed spot, full of imperishable associations, it is proposed to re-establish a monastery for the residence of Bhikkhus representing the Buddhist countries of Tibet, Ceylon, China, Japan, Cambodia, Burmah, Chittagong, Nepal, Korea, and Arakan. We hope to found also a college at Buddha Gaya for training young men of unblemished character, of whatsoever race and country, for the Buddhist Order (Sangha), on the lines of the ancient Buddhist University at

Nalanda, where were taught the "Mahayana and also works belonging to the eighteen sects.'

"The study of Sanskrit, Pali and English will be made compulsory on all students. One or more Buddhist scholars from each of the Buddhist countries will in time be attached to the staff of teachers.

"To carry on this great and glorious work of Buddhist revival, after a torpor of seven hundred years, whence dates the destruction of Buddhism in India, the Maha Bodhi Society has been organised, and the promoters solicit sympathy and generous support all the world over."

In brief, the primary purpose of the Society was to reclaim the Great Maha Bodhi Temple, and to establish a Buddhist monastery there so as to preserve the sanctity of the most sacred Buddhist shrine. The Society also planned to work for the revival of Buddhism in India, the land of its birth.

After founding the Society, Dharmapala thought of re-establishing the Sangha at Buddha Gaya on the coming fullmoon day of the month of Asadha, the day on which Lord Buddha had preached His First Sermon at Sarnath. With this object in view, he appealed to the Bhikkhus of Sri Lanka, and succeeded in obtaining four monks. Dunuwila Chandjoti, Matale Sumangala, Anuradhapura Pemananda and Galle Sudassana. Accompanied by them, he reached Buddha Gaya on the eve of the Asadha fullmoon day and reverently hoisted next morning the Buddhist flag under the Bodhi Tree. Elated on seeing the Buddhist flag on the sacred spot, Dharmapala recorded in his diary as under:

> "Ah, how beautifully it flutters in the moonlight breeze! May the mission be a success! I hope and sincerely trust that the priests may be a light to the people and will lead a life of purity, and show the people of India the intrinsic merits of our holy religion."

Having installed the four Buddhist monks in the Burmese Rest House, Dharmapala approached the Mahant for the purchase of a plot of land for the Maha Bodhi Society's office but he was greatly distressed to find the delaying tactics of the Mahant and the indifferent attitude of the Collector of Gaya. Hurt by this obstructive attitude, Dharmapala decided to organize an International Buddhist Conference at Buddha Gaya. This Conference, first of its kind on Indian soil after centuries of darkness, was held on 31 October 1891. The representatives from Sri Lanka, China, Japan and Chittagong attended this Conference, and promised full support to Anagarika in his struggle to regain the control of the sacred Maha Bodhi Temple.

Later, Anagarika Dharmapala shifted to Calcutta, where the home of a large-hearted businessman, Neel Comul Mookerjee, became his home. In May 1892, Dharmapala founded the Maha Bodhi journal the first of its kind in India. In its first issue, Dharmapala wrote:

> "The Maha Bodhi Society has commenced its mission for the resuscitation of Buddhism in the land of its birth, and within these eleven months the movement has been received with great sympathy. Since the commencement of our labours only words of encouragement have been received from all parts of the learned world.
>
> "The hope of man is man.
>
> I would not let one cry when I would save." said Sakya Muni. The encouragement we have received gives us hope to push forward."

While Dharmapala was staying in Calcutta and working with 'unflagging zeal and tireless energy' for the cause for which he had dedicated his life, hostile winds were blowing at Buddha Gaya. In January 1893, when Col Olcott arrived in Calcutta, they decided to visit Buddha Gaya. On their arrival at Buddha Gaya on 4 February, they found that the previous evening the Mahant's men had severely beaten up two of the monks, Bhikkhu Sumangala and another while they were peacefully engaged in reading the scriptures. Horrified by this unprovoked attack, Col. Olcott at once met the Mahant to find out the reasons for this cowardly act. Saying that he had ownership rights on the entire property at Bodh Gaya, the Mahant objected to the presence of the monks. He also refused either to sell or lease the land on any terms, or to allow the Buddhists to erect a Rest House for the pilgrims. Meanwhile, Ven. Sumangala was admitted in the hospital, and a criminal case was filled by Dharmapala against the assailants. Ven. Sumangala, however, thought otherwise. From the hospital bed he sent an application to the police that neither he nor his fellow monks could be witnesses to the case and thus cause their assailants to be punished. On going through this application, the District Superintendent of Police is said to have remarked that 'I always thought these Indian priests made a living out of religion. These Buddhist priests from Ceylon actually practise it."

In July 1893, Dharmapala, after entrusting the journal to Sarat Chandra Das, left for America to attend the World Parliament of Religions, to be held at Chicago in September, to which he had been invited as the representative of the Theravada Buddhists. On his way to America, Dharmapala spent some time in London where he was welcomed by Sir Edwin Arnold, and others. At the Parliament of World Religions, the first of its kind to be held anywhere in the World, Dharmapala presented his paper, "The World's Debt to Buddha" written in simple but forceful and lucid language, in so gracious and dignified manner that it made profound influence on the audience.

The Parliament of Religions ended on 27 September 1893. After delivering a few more lectures in America, Dharmapala sailed for India via Japan. A chance meeting with Mrs. Mary Foster, a wealthy lady of Honolulu, on board the S.S. Oceanic at Honolulu on 18 October 1893 proved of immense significance as Mrs Foster later became the greatest benefactor of the Maha Bodhi Society.

From Honolulu, Dharmapala moved further, and reached Yokohama in Japan, where he was cordially received. In Japan, he managed to procure a beautiful Buddha statue which he wanted to enshrine in the upper chamber of the sacred Maha Bodhi Temple. The story of this gift from the Japanese people was later described by Anagarika Dharmapala as follows:

> "When I was in Tokyo last November, I told the Rev. S. Asahi, Chief Priest of the Tentoku-ji Temple that the image of Maya Devi which is now enshrined on the altar of the upper storey of the Great Temple at Buddha Gaya could be replaced by a statue of Buddha if we had one from Japan, and am glad that he was successful in getting a historic image of the Great Teacher about seven hundred years old. This beautiful image, two feet high, represents Buddha sitting on the lotus seat in the process of expounding the Law. It was carved by the order of the great general who erected the famous Kamakura statue of Buddha, and it remained enshrined these seven hundred years in the temple in Kanagawa near Yokohama."

After his long foreign tour, Anagarika Dharmapala returned to Calcutta on 31 March 1894. And on 11 April, he went to Gaya with an intention to install the beautiful Buddha image, gifed by the Japanese Buddhists, in the upper chamber of Maha Bodhi Temple. When however, he met the Collector of Gaya, he advised him 'to win over the Hindu opinion to his side in the first instance. He accordingly went to Banaras and met the Brahmin leaders. The orthodox Hindus not only opposed his proposal of installing the Buddha image in the Maha Bodhi Temple, which they claimed was a Hindu temple because Buddha was an incarnation of Vishnu, but also threatened him with dire consequences in case he tired to do so of his own. In view of this, Dharmapala postponed the installation for some time. Unmindful of these threats, however, Dharmapala decided to install the Buddha image of his own after a few months. It was on 25 February 1895. Dharmapala records in his diary:

> "At 2 in the morning I woke up and sat in meditation for a little time and then my mind suggested, as it did yesterday under the Bodhi Tree, to take the Japanese Image to the Maha Bodhi Temple. I woke up the priests and then asked them to sit in contemplation for a time. Then it was decided that we should take the Image early morning from Gaya to Buddha Gaya. In silence I vowed 7 times giving up my life for the Buddha's sake. Before dawn we packed the image and by 7 were off to Buddha Gaya. Soon after our arrival at Buddha Gaya, the boxes containing the Image were taken upstairs to the Maha Bodhi Temple and when we were going to light candles, the Mahant's gosains came up and threatened me to remove the Image. Oh, it was painful indeed. Buddhists are not allowed to worship in their own Temple."

Finding Dharmapala reluctant to remove the Image, the Mahant's men, who were forty-fifty in number, assaulted him and other monks, and threw out the Buddha Image in the courtyard. The Buddha Image was later kept by Dharmapala in the Burmese Rest House. Surprisingly, the Collector of Gaya, representing the British Government, ordered in April 1896 the Maha Bodhi Society to have the image removed from the Rest House, otherwise, the order said, it would be removed by Government. However, good sense prevailed later, and the unworthy order was rescinded.

Then, in 1897, the Mahant and some Hindu organisations, in particular, the British India Association, to their eternal shame, represented to the Government that the Buddha image should be removed from the Rest House as "It was offensive to the Hindus." Luckily, the Government did not yield to the request.

In the meanwhile, a criminal case had been filed by Anagarika Dharmapala against the Mahant's men for assaulting him and the bhikkhus on 25 February 1895. Finding the miscreants guilty, the Magistrate of Gaya, sentenced them to one month's simple imprisonment and imposed a fine of one hundred rupees each. This judgment was upheld by the District Court to which the assailants had appealed. Though the crucial question of the ownership of the Maha Bodhi Temple was not decided by the court on the plea that the parties should go to the Civil Court as it is only that Court which can decide the question of title, yet the District Judge of Gaya in his judgment observed that the Maha Bodhi Temple was entirely a Buddhist shrine. He pronounced:

> "(a) The temple has continually and regularly been used as a Buddhist place of worship by Buddhist pilgrims (b) No form of Hindu worship has been carried on inside the Maha Bodhi Temple and there is nothing to show that any such has been carried on in it for many centuries, if ever, since Sankara's attempt. But since July of last year there has undoubtedly been an attempt at the instance of the Mahant and his disciples to carry on a semblance of Hindu worship of the great image of the Buddha which is on the altar of the Sanctum on the ground floor of the temple. Since then, as deposed by the custodian a Brahmin priest named Bishnu Misra has been employed who passes a light in front of the image, sounds bells, laves the image and altar and a tilak or Hindu caste mark has been painted on the forehead and the image clothed with a regular vestment and the head decked with flowers. The Custodian who is a Kulin Brahmin of the highest caste deposes that nevertheless what is done does not constitute complete Hindu worship, and it must be remembered that in spite of this neither the Mahant nor any of his disciples nor any Hindu has ever been seen by him worshipping inside the temple. All the Hindu worship started last year, it will be observed, shortly after Dharmapala endeavoured to place the Japanese image in the temple, and on a review of the evidence there is no room for reasonable doubt that it is of specious kind started as a mere strategem for giving the Mahant a pretext for interfering with the dealings of the Buddhists with the temple and strengthening whatever prescriptive rights he may possess to the usufruct of the offerings made at it?"

This was a substantial gain for the Society. However, when the matter went up before the two Judges of the Calcutta High Court they sided with the orthodoxy; quashed the sentence, and refunded the fine saying that "the assailants represented the interests of the Mahant."

Anagarika Dharmapala's Epic Struggle and his confrontation with the powerful Hindu Mahant in the initial stages was described in brief in

January 1906 issue of the Maha Bodhi journal, under the title "A Retrospect," by some of the helpers of the Anagarika. According to them:

> "Started under very poor patronage the Maha Bodhi Society began its romantic career in a strange land, and notwithstanding stupendous obstacles the movement was pushed one.
>
> Hostile manifestations began to materialise in realistic forms and the first sledge hammer attack that we received was in February 1893 when our Bhikkhus were mercilessly assaulted by the Mahant's men at Buddha Gaya. These Bhikkhus were removed from Buddha Gaya to Gaya on the advice of Colonel Olcott and we lost our hold at Buddha Gaya. In the meanwhile negotiations were made to purchase the Maha Bodhi village. Things were in a precarious state when the General Secretary left India to attend the Chicago Parliament in July 1893. It was a special invitation that he received from the Chairman, all expenses of the round trip being paid by the Congress Committee. The Journal was left in the hands of Rai Bahadur Sarat Chandra Das and Mr. Charu Chandra Bose. The Bhikkhus were not allowed to return to Buddha Gaya for fear of the Hindu Mahant.
>
> The visit of the General Secretary to America was productive of good results, inasmuch as his presence with the American people. Millions for the first time came to know of the ethics of the great Religion. Buddhism met with a triumphant success at the Parliament and the General Secretary left Chicago for India via Japan.
>
> In Japan he was received with cordial greetings by the Japanese Buddhists and by Members of the Japan Maha Bodhi Society. He explained to them the situation of affairs at Buddha Gaya and as a token of their appreciation of his services the beautiful historic Image of Buddha was presented to the Maha Bodhi Temple at Buddha Gaya.
>
> In 1894 May the Great Image was to have been installed in the Shrine room at Buddha Gaya. All arrangements were complete, and at the Twelfth hour the Mahanth exhibited hostile feelings and prevented our entrance. The Bhikkhus and the Image were forbidden entrance within the precincts of Maha-Bodhi Temple; and they were obliged to remain at Gaya in-charge of the Image. The negotiations for the purchase of the Maha Bodhi land were being carried on, a lac (100000) of rupees was required and the General

Secretary began his campaign in Ceylon to raise the Maha Bodhi Fund. In three months Rs. 38,000 were raised.

Things were moving on beautifully, but an unexpected cataclysm occurred. The General Secretary in the early morning of the 24th February 1895 was implied to take the Image from Gaya to Buddha Gaya. Contrary to expectations he met with no resistance at the Temple and the Image was enshrined on the upper storey of the Temple.

Then followed the explosion. The myrmidons of the Hindu Mahant came armed and threatened the party of 4 Buddhists and forcibly carried away the beautiful Image and placed it on the open square before the Temple. The Bhikkhus in the meanwhile regained entrance to their old quarters and took possession of the Burmese Rest House; the General Secretary under advice of the Patna Commissioner instituted legal proceedings, Colonel Olcott came over to Calcutta to inquire into the matter and telegraphed to the Ceylon Society that the case must proceed on, and the great Buddha Gaya Temple case was the result. It cost the Mahant Rs. 100,000 and the Buddhists had to expend Rs. 23,000. The Mahant contending to make the Temple a Hindu Shrine the M.B.S. combatting the views of the Mahant's lawyers; showing that it was never converted into a Hindu Temple. The Viceroy Lord Elgin visited the Temple a few days after the disturbance and directed the removal of the Japanese Image to the Burmese Rest House. Under Police escort the Image was placed in the Burmese Rest House and there it still lies enshrined guarded by the Bhikkhu M.P. Saumangala.

The Temple Case was a big affair, all over India people came to know of the Buddhist revival and of the Maha Bodhi Society and the High Court decided that the Temple was never converted into a Hindu Shrine and that it is a Buddhist Temple. This was a great gain to the Buddhists. The Japanese Image decided the situation of affairs; and the Buddhists secured a permanent foothold at Buddha Gaya and got back their lost Rest House built by the late King Mindon Min of Burma. Two years more the rights of occupancy would have been confirmed and the Mahant become absolute master; but the case destroyed all his anticipations and the Buddhists triumphed. There is still room for instituting a civil case against the Mahant; it only required money and we hope that the good Buddhists who love their religion will come forward and contest this point at some future time.

Before the case the Mahant was the dominating lord of the place. Hundreds of men were ready to carry out his orders, plans were matured to kill Dharmapala, Buddhist Bhikkhus were assaulted when they attempted to remain permanently at Buddha-Gaya; the Burmese Rest House was claimed as his property,, no one dared to remonstrate against his orders. The case settled all in favour of the Buddhists. The Mahant was brought to his senses, his absolute power was challenged and the Buddhists regained their lost place. What a change.!

The Buddhists expended Rs. 23,000 and got back their lost prestige which is worth more than a million and secured the Burmese Rest House which is worth to the Buddhists over a hundred thousand rupees, the amount spent by the late King to secure this site, and the M.B.S. got the Government to get land to build the new Maha Bodhi Dharmasala.

To gain all this the General Secretary had to work risking his life; for full ten years he exerted strenuously to gain a foothold at Buddha Gaya. The Government of Bengal was opposed to the Buddhists at first. Chief Secretary Cotton was a declared enemy of the Buddhists. His son was Mahant's legal advisor and we were greatly harassed by the former. But his successors were very friendly and also the Lieut. Governors, Sir Alexander Mackenzie and Sir John Woodburn. Messers Bolton Buckland, Bourdillon, Macpherson, Oldham showed a spirit of sympathy in our efforts.

All through this mighty struggle a few friends remained firm. On behalf of the Buddhists we thank sincerely Messrs Norendo Nath Sen, Neel Comal Mookerjee, Nanda Kishore Lall, Mahesh Narayan, Sachchidananda Sinha, Hari Dass Chatterjee, Durga Shanker Bhattacharjee, C.C. Bose, Rai Bahadurs Sarat Chandra Das and J.D. Mazumdar.

For fourteen years we have laboured with devotion to the cause. Mistakes we have made, but no great work can ever be accomplished without the sacrifice of life, limb and wealth. A few Buddhists had been hostile to us in Burma, Siam, Japan, Arakan and Ceylon. But we patiently and cheerfully persevered with the conviction that ours was a just cause. We were maligned and slandered maliciously but with the ideal example of patience of our Blessed

Lord before us we harboured no anger in our hearts. Truth and Humanity is our motto and we shall exert to work in accordance with these at all times even at the risk of our life."

Dharmapala's battle against the mighty Mahant of Bodh Gaya received a set back when Mahant's suit filed in 1906, for the ejection of the Buddhist monks from the Burmese Rest House, on the plea that the Rest House was his property, was accepted by the District Court. As the High Court also upheld the lower court's judgment, the Maha Bodhi Society was temporarily ousted from the Rest House in February 1910. Undaunted, however, Dharmapala continued the struggle.

In 1922, when Dharmapala was away in Sri Lanka, Valisinha alongwith Ven. K. Srinivasa Nayaka Thera attended the Gaya Congress Session in order to bring to the notice of the delegates the problem of the Buddha Gaya Temple. Here, Rahul Sankrityayan (then known as Baba Ramodardas) was a member of the Bihar Provincial Congress Committee, played a leading role in getting the Temple question taken up by the Congress. Later when a Committee to go into the Buddha Gaya Temple question was appointed by the Congress under the Chairmanship of Dr. Rajendra Prasad, Valisinha and P.P. Siriwardene represented the Society on the Committee.

The Rajendra Prasad Committee recommended inter-alia that a Committee of five Buddhists and five Hindus should be constituted and management and control of the temple should be left to it. Ultimately, however, nothing came out of this Committee's report as even the mild recommendation that equal number of Buddhists and Hindus should manage the Temple was not accepted by the Mahant.

However, the Buddha Gaya Temple question aroused the conscience of many Hindus, and they forcefully supported the Buddhist cause. When the matter was still under the consideration of the Rajendra Prasad Committee, appointed by the Congress Committee, Mahatma Gandhi wrote in the 'Young India' as under:

> "The reader will remember that a movement has been in progress for some years for the restoration to Buddhists of the great and historic temple at Buddha Gaya. But it seems to have made no tangible headway. At the Cocanada Congress Babu Rajendra Prasad was appointed to inquire into the matter and report. He had not been able to do so up to the time of the meeting. A Buddhist deputation came from Ceylon to Belgaum during the Congress week to plead the Buddhistic cause personally before the Congress. . . ."

> "...The only thing, therefore, the committee was able to do was to ask Rajendra Babu to hasten and let the Working Committee have his report on or before the end of the present month.
>
> "There is no doubt that the possession of the Temple should vest in the Buddhists. There may be legal difficulties. They must be overcome. If the report is true that animal sacrifice is offered in the temple, it is a sacrilege. It is equally a sacrilege if the worship is offered, as it is alleged, in a way calculated to wound the susceptibilities of Buddhists. We should take pride in helping the restoration of the temple to its rightful trustees. I hope Rajendra Babu will secure all the literature on the subject and produce a report which can serve as a guide for all who wish to advance the cause of the Buddhist claimants."

Gurudev Rabindranath Tagore was another great supporter of the Buddhist case. He said:

> "I am sure it will be admitted by all Hindus who are true to their own ideals, that it is an intolerable wrong to allow the temple raised on the spot where Lord Buddha attained his enlightenment, to remain under the control of a rival sect which can neither have an intimate knowledge of nor sympathy for the Buddhist religion and its rites of worship. I consider it to be a sacred duty for all individuals believing in freedom and justice to help restore this historical site to the community of people who still reverentially carry on that particular current of history in their own living faith...."

Many more enlightened Hindus supported the Buddhist claim over the Buddha Gaya Temple. Deshbandhu C.R. Das said, "In my opinion, the Buddha Gaya Temple belongs to the Buddhists." And Pandit Vibhusekhara Bhattacharya observed: "Let us, the Hindus, dispassionately consider the question of the Buddha Gaya Temple in the heart of our hearts and the truth will be revealed that it is the Buddhists who are more deserving than ourselves to take possession of the shrine."

Apart from "regaining the control of the Great Maha Bodhi Temple and developing Buddha Gaya as a living Buddhist shrine, the Anagarika was also keen to develop the holy Isipatana, Sarnath as a living shrine. Here he was more successful as he was dealing with the British who were sympathetic, and not the Mahant of Bodh Gaya, who was greedy and callous, not caring for the sentiments of the Buddhists. At Sarnath, Dharmapala acquired the required land for a befitting Vihara, the foundation stone of which was laid in 1922. The construction work thereon, however, had to be suspended as the Archaeological Survey of India had certain reservations in regard to its location. After negotiations, the Government not only allotted an alternative piece of land but also agreed to set apart about 20 acres of land, and to develop the same as a park at their cost as annexe to the Vihara. Consequently, the construction of the Vihara was started again in 1927, and the magnificent Mulagandhakuti Vihara, with ancient Buddhist architectural decorations carved on red stone, was completed in 1931.

In 1929, Dharmapala returned to Sri Lanka and fell seriously ill. For the next three years he was confined to bed with stomach trouble and heart disease. In the meanwhile, his only surviving brother, Dr. C.A. Hewavitarne, who was of great help to him after the demise of his father, died in a tragic railway accident in 1929. Then in December 1930, his foster mother, Mrs. Mary E. Foster, passed away. For Anagarika's living, the main financial support came from his family — father, mother and brother — and for his other activities, particularly the buildings, his greatest benefactor was Mrs. Foster of Honolulu, who has often been ranked with Anathapindka and Visakha of Buddha's time.

In spite of these irreparable losses, Dharmapala through sheer will-power recovered enough to undertake sea journey to Calcutta. At the end of March 1931, he reached Sarnath and began directing the affairs of the Society once again. He also brought to Sarnath a batch of ten samaneras from Sri Lanka, who he thought after training would be able to continue his efforts of propagating the Dhamma in India.

Having spent his entire life as Anagarika or homeless wanderer, Dharmapala decided to take a step further on the road to Nirvana. On 13 July 1931 he took the Pabbajja or lower ordination from Ven. Borug-gamuwe Rewata Thera and received the name of Sri Devamitta Dham-mapala as Bhikkhu. Anagarika Dharmapala completed his life-long mission by consecrating the magnificent Mulagandhakuti Vihara at Sarnath on 11 November 1931 (Kartika Purnima).

The opening of the Mulagandhakuti Vihara was an important mile-stone in the history of modern Buddhism. It's completion was also the most glorious achievement of Anagarika Dharmapala, after 40 years of his labours for the revival of Buddhism in India.

In December 1932, Dharmapala again fell seriously ill, and wishing to die as a full member of the Sangha he received the Upasampada or higher ordination on 16 January 1933. On receiving higher ordination,

Dharmapala felt greatly relieved of all the worries, and looked serene and calm. But within a couple of months his health took a serious turn.

Even at his death-bed, Anagarika Dharmapala was thinking of the Buddha Gaya Temple. In fact, he was sad and sorrowful as he could not fulfil his mission of liberating the Great Temple from the clutches of the Hindu Mahant. He was more pained when even some Buddhist Societies tried to sabotage his efforts for selfish ends. Devapriya Valisinha, who was to the Anagarika what Ananda was to the Buddha, records an incident which happened on 24 April 1933, just five days before Dharmapala breathed his last, which shows that when he saw his end coming near, he talked more and more of the Buddha Gaya Temple. Valisinha writes as follows in June 1933 issue of the Maha Bodhi Journal."

> "On receiving news of his serious illness the Samaneras who were sent to Buddha Gaya, returned on the 24th and peeped into the sick room. "From where are they coming?", enquired Venerable Dhammapala. "From Buddha Gaya", replied Revd. Sasanasiri who was standing closeby. When he heard this there was quite an agitated look in his face giving an index to the worrying emotions in his heart and then at last he asked to every one's surprise, "When her child is dying will the mother run away?" Those present readily understood what he meant was that Buddha Gaya was of greater importance to him than his own life. Throughout his illness Venerable Dhammapala kept harping on the Buddha Gaya question. Not a day passed without a reference to it. It had been his greatest ambition to recover the sacred site for the Buddhist world. Lately, he had re-started the movement and was contemplating a vigorous campaign when he unfortunately fell ill. "If I live another two years I shall see that the Holy Temple is restored," he told me once. His plan was to take residence at Buddha Gaya itself and from there carry on his last battle. He expected the whole Buddhist world to stand by him like one man, but in this he was sadly mistaken. It was a rude awakening that he received a copy of a memorial sent by the Congress of Buddhist Associations dealing a death blow to his life's long aspirations. It was the greatest shock of his life and I can vividly recollect his pain and anguish when he read it. Alas, he never recovered from this shock. How could he forget such treachery even on his sick bed?"

Anagarika Dharmapala breathed his last at Sarnath on 29 April 1933, and Devapriya Valisinha, his most devoted and trusted Assistant succeeded him as General Secretary of the Maha Bodhi Society of India. Since 1922, Valisinha had been associated with the movement for regaining this holy temple from the Mahant. He kept on raising this question at every forum which he thought could help in finding a solution. In 1935, he attended the Kanpur Session of the Hindu Maha Sabha presided over by Bhikkhu Ottama of Burma and raised this question in the Subjects Committee. After a great deal of hesitation, a Committee was appointed. Valisinha appeared before the Committee. This Committee also commended the appointment of a Joint Managing Committee. The Mahant left the decision to the Sankaracarya of Puri, who vehemently opposed the recommendations. Thus, the matter ended in stalemate, and it remained so till India attained Independence on 15 August 1947.

Chapter XIV

THE BODH GAYA TEMPLE ACT, 1949

The Buddha Gaya Temple question that had agitated the minds of the Buddhists and Hindus alike since 1891 took a favourable turn after India attained Independence on 15 August 1947. With the adoption of the Buddhist symbols: the Dhamma Wheel, and the Lion-Capital of the Asokan Pillar at Sarnath, as the National Symbols of Free India, Buddhism came to be associated with nationalism and ancient Indian culture.

After independence, National Governments came to be formed in all the Provinces. As the luck would have it, Dr. Srikrishna Sinha, who was a great admirer of the Buddha, became the first Prime Minister (later designated as Chief Minister) of Bihar. When approached by Devapriya Valisinha, General Secretary of the Maha Bodhi Society of India, to help in the transfer of the management of the Buddha Gaya Temple to the Buddhists, Dr. Sinha readily agreed to do so. And in October, 1948, he introduced the Bodh Gaya Temple Bill in the Bihar Legislative Assembly. However, the Bill, as introduced, did not meet the aspirations of the Buddhists as in the proposed Management Committee the Hindus were to have majority, and not the Buddhists. Hence, the Bill was vehemently criticised by the Maha Bodhi Society, and it reiterated its demand that the Buddhists should be given majority in the Temple Management Committee. But there was no response from the Government of Bihar. Making a last minute appeal to the Bihar Legislative Assembly to reconsider the matter, Valisinha pleaded as follows in the May 1949 issue of the Maha Bodhi Journal:

> "The Select Committee appointed by the Bihar Legsilative Assembly to consider the proposed Bill has submitted its report and the Bill, as amended by the Committee, is most likely to go through the Legislature before the 12th this month (May), the auspicious

day of Lord Buddha's birth. We are gratified to find that at least a few of the changes suggested by our Society have been accepted although the most vital one with regard to the composition of the Managing Committee has not been considered at all. While we reiterate the just and reasonable Buddhist claim to a majority of seats in the Managing Committee, we shall fail in our duty if we do not give expression to our appreciation of the Select Committee's action in recommending the formation of an Advisory Board with a majority of Buddhists who may not all be Indians. This is a step in the right direction and, although the function of the Board is to tender advice which may or may not be accepted by the Managing Committee, its advice is bound to carry weight. We, therefore, heartily welcome this provision in the Bill. The other changes proposed are: (1) Setting up of the Committee's office at Buddha Gaya itself instead of at Gaya, and (2) The inclusion of Vajrasana and Bodhi Tree in the term 'temple,' thus bringing these two important objects of Buddhist veneration more specially within the jurisdiction of the Committee.

While we congratulate the Select Committee on the above changes, we are constrained to confess that we still feel that the failure to give the Buddhists a majority in the Managing Committee is a mistake of the first magnitude. As Mr. J.C. Mathur, District Magistrate of Gaya, who is himself a devout Hindu, rightly points out in his letter published on another page, this is an unnecessary irritant to the Buddhists which could have been easily avoided. After all the number of Buddhists in India is so small and none at Buddha Gaya itself, even with a majority they would be entirely at the mercy of the surrounding Hindu population without whose good-will and co-operation, such a Committee could never function. Therefore, it would have been a more gracious and magnanimous act on the part of the Hindu Legislators, had it been possible for them to meet Buddhist wishes fully in this respect. For their reluctance to give a majority to the Buddhists, they may, of course, have their own reasons and weighty ones too—but we have not been enlightened on the matter. We earnestly trust that, even at this late hours, it will be possible for them to reconsider the constitution of the Managing Committee."

Ignoring the pleas made by the Maha Bodhi Society of India, and other Buddhists, the Draft Bill giving majority to the Hindus in the

Management Committee was passed by the Bihar Legislative Assembly in May 1949. In accordance with the Bodh Gaya Temple Act, 1949, a copy of which may please be seen in Appendix, the Management and control of the Temple, the temple land and the properties appertaining thereto, was to be entrusted to a committee of four Buddhists and four Hindus, including the Mahant, with the District Magistrate of Gaya (who must always be a Hindu) as Chairman. Though not a very happy solution yet it was something for which the Buddhists had to fight for nearly sixty years.

The enactment of the Bodh Gaya Temple Act in May 1949 incidentally coincided with the Buddha Jayanti in that year. As per directions of Dr. Srikrishna Sinha, the Buddha Jayanti celebrations were organised in a big way for the first time at Buddha Gaya, the very site where the Buddha had attained supreme enlightenment. As interesting report on this historic Buddha Jayanti function was published on 14 May 1949, in Search Light, Patna. This is how the correspondent describes this function:

> "To use very un-spriritual language Gautama Buddha performed a hattrick in this day though unlike many prophets he was clean, rational and completely free from the nonsense of miracles and mysteries. He was born, he attained enlightenment, he died the same day—Vaishakha Purnima. To the superstitious it is bound to appear a highly divine coincidence.
>
> Since in India the faithful attach more importance to outward symbol than to inward grace, this triple coincidence has held a meaning all its own and so anything betwen thirty and forty thousand people managed to reach Bodh Gaya on Thursday, May 12, to witness the bones of the Lord, to go round the temple, and to hear the orators in action.
>
> The one reason why there were so many big crowds on the scene was the procession on the morning of Thursday. It attracted crowds right from the start. A craze spread among the people soon and they mustered in large numbers for an evening function, even as their forefathers did in the days of Buddha. The decorated car in which the Buddha relices were carried was a piece of art.
>
> It was a lovely scene at the Bodhi Tree, where the relics were solemnly deposited and a puja began—the tree under which the Enlightenment took place. Buddhism being a mass religion did not discard idolatry. Yet it is inconceivable how the severe rationale of

the Buddhist faith could square with this practice. As bhikkhus from Tibet and Ceylon began to offer worship, I began to wonder whether Buddha belonged to their countries or ours. Profound thanks are due to them for their enthusiasm and for their attempts to rekindle the faith in the Indian mind. Most of them frankly confessed to me, as they also did sometime ago, in Patna, that they were surprised at the response of the populace to the reawakening of the Buddhist faith. It is now our problem to put Hinduism and Buddhism together and make the best of them.

As people, specially women with children in arms, passed in a single row around the platform where the Buddha bones were on exhibition, it presented an inspiring scene to watch. There was a lot of difference, however, between this occasion and the last when we saw the relics of Buddha's disciples in our museum. I had to apply the microscope to my eyes this time to make sure that I was really seeing something at Gaya.''

THE WEATHER

The weather was delightful. It was evidently determined to behave in a quiet, Buddhistic fashion. It was not even sultry. A cool wind kept blowing all the time. And only when the proceedings of the evening had been over, did the skies, as if overjoyed, released torrents of flood. Some may have missed the latter part of the Punch and Judy sort of shows that were being put on board but we did not miss our gala six-course dinner. Only when the last morsel of food had been swallowed, did rain drops began to pelt us severely. I started by saying something about Buddha being no miracle-worker, I think last night he was one, otherwise, the whole function might have ended in sorry disaster.

STATE FUNCTION

It was a State function through and through, the arrangements being in the hands of officials of the Government of Bihar: Patna was well represented. The messages for the occasion were optimistic, Rajendra Babu confidently looking forward to a re-emergence of the religion of love and peace. We missed Governor Aney, but the Prime Minister Dr. Sri Krishna Sinha, carried everything before him. The speeches were all on a high note, talking about an international university at Gaya, making India the centre of a new illumination, making Buddhism the foundation of a modern society. I liked most the learned discourse of a Pandit from North Bihar. He was overflowing with Brahminism and Sanskrit. He represented a tradition that has driven Buddhism out of India and condemned Buddha's Magadha as a sin-infested place. He spoke appreciatively of the Buddhist philosophy and wanted increased opportunities for a critical study of the two faiths with a view to harmonising.

The Prime Minister in his speech covered the territory from Magadha to mankind. He appeared by now to be a convinced Buddhist. At one time he was so eloquent that I thought he was making Buddha a local Magadha hero. But what actually he did was to tell the Magadha people to be so many instruments for the revaluation of the Buddhist faith that had its origin here, and its elevation to a higher status in the story of mankind. That indeed, is the real attitude for those to take up who hope to build a new Asia on the secure foundations of a common faith that leaps over physical boundaries and the limitations of mere belief and stirs us to deeds of valiant action in integral defence of human rights.''

Search Light, Patna.

While the Bihar Government was congratulating itself for having passed the Bodh Gaya Temple Bill, and the Buddhists were also a bit happy to get at least partial control over the Maha Bodhi Temple but the Mahant was very much distressed. As the Temple was a major source of income for him, the Mahant wanted to cling to it as long as possible. Hence, he filed a writ in the Supreme Court requesting the Court to declare the Bodh Gaya Temple Act as a violation of the Constitution of India. He even succeeded in obtaining an injunction from the Magistrate at Gaya, preventing the Government from taking over the Temple and entrusting its management to a Committee in accordance with the 1949 Act. As a result of such obstructive tactics of the Mahant, the Government of Bihar could not take over the Temple and entrust its management to a Committee as envisaged in the Act, for nearly three years, and it was only towards the end of 1952 that the first Management Committee was constituted.

APPENDIX

THE BODH GAYA TEMPLE ACT, 1949

(BIHAR ACT 17 OF 1949)

(as modified up to the 8th February, 1955)

[Governor's assent published in the Bihar Gazette of the 6th July, 1949].

An Act to make provision for the better management of the Bodh Gaya Temple and the properties appertaining thereto.

Whereas it is expedient to make provision for the better management of the Bodh Gaya Temple and properties appertaining thereto.

It is hereby enacted as follows:

Short title and Commencement — 1. (1) This Act may be called the Bodh Gaya Temple Act, 1949

(2) It shall come into force at once.

Definition — 2. In this Act, unless there is anything repugnant in the subject or context,—

(a) "The temple" means the great temple built by the site of the Mahabodhi Tree near the village of Bodh Gaya in the district of Gaya and includes the Mahabodhi Tree and Vajrasana:[1]

(b) "The temple land" means the land in which the temple and its precincts stand and shall cover such area or shall lie within such boundaries as the [2] State Government may, by notification direct;

(c) "The Mahanth" means the presiding priest for the time being of Saivite Monastery at Bodh Gaya; and

(d) "Committee" means the Committee constituted under Section 3.

Constitution of Committee — 3. (1) As soon as may be after the commencement of this the [2]: [State] Government shall constitute a Committee as hereinafter provided and entrust it with the management and control of the temple, the temple land and the properties appertaining thereto.

(Secs. 4-6)

(2) The Committee Shall consist of a Chairman and eight members nominated by the [1] [State] Government, all of whom shall be Indians and of whom

1 Legislative Papers,—For statement of Objects and Reasons, See the Bihar Gazette, 1949, Pt. V, p 230; for proceedings in the Legislative Assembly, see the Bihar Legislative Assembly Debates, 1948, Vol. V, No. 12, pp. 14-36; 1949, Vol VI, No. 32, pp. 31-61 and Vol. VI, No. 48, pp. 41-44 and for proceedings in the Legislative Council, see the Bihar Legilative Council Debates, 1948, Vol XI, No. 32, pp. 16-40.

2 Subs. by para. 4 (1) of the A.L.O. for "Provincial".

four shall be Buddhists and four shall be Hindus including the Mahant:

Provided that if the Mahant is a minor or of unsound mind or refuses to serve on the Committee, another Hindu member shall be nominated in his place.

(3) The District Magistrate of Gaya shall be the ex-officio Chairman of Committee:

Provided that the [1] [State] Government shall nominate a Hindu as Chairman of the Committee for the period during which the District Magistrate of Gaya is non-Hindu.

(4) The [1]·[State] Government shall nominate a person from among the members to act as Secretary of the Committee.

Incorporation of Committee.

4. The Committee shall be a body corporate by the name of the Bodh Gaya Temple Management Committee, having perpetual succession and a common seal, with power to acquire and hold property, both movable and immovable, and to contract, and shall by the said name sue or be sued.

Term of office of members.

5. (1) The term of office of the members of the Committee shall be three years:

Provided that the [1] [State] Government, if they are satisfied that the Committee is guilty of gross mismanagement, dissolve the Committee and constitute another Committee or assume direct control of the temple, temple land and the properties appertaining thereto.

(2) Where a member of Committee dies, resigns, refuses to serve on the Committee, absents himself from six consecutive meetings of the Committee, without the leave of the Committee or ceases to reside in India, or becomes incapable of working, the [1] [State] Government may nominate a person to fill the vacancy.

(3) Any Act done by the Committee shall not be questioned on the ground merely of the existence

1 Subs. by para. 4 (1) of the A.L.O for "Provincial."

of any vacancy in or any defect in the constitution of the Committee.

Publication of names of Chariman and members.

6. The name of the Chariman other than the District Magistrate of Gaya and of every member of the Committee shall be published by the [1]: [State] Government in the Official Gazette,

(Secs. 7-10)

Office and meetings of the Committee.

7. (1) The Committee shall maintain its office at Bodh Gaya.

(2) At the meeting of the Committee the Chairman, or in his absense one of the members to be elected at the meeting, shall preside.

(3) No business shall be transacted at any meeting unless at least four members are present.

Limitation on Committee's power to alienate property.

8. (1) No movable property of a non-perishable nature appertaining to the temple shall be transferred without the previous sanction of the Committee, and, if the value of the property is more than one thousand rupees, without the previous approval of the[1] [State] Government.

(2) No immovable property appertaining to the temple shall be leased for more than three years or mortgaged, sold or otherwise alienated except with the previous sanction of the Committee and the [1] [State] Government.

Limitation of borrowing power.

9. The Committee shall have no power to borrow money from any person except with the previous sanction of the[1] [State] Government.

Duties of the Committee.

10. Subject to the provisions of this Act or of any rules made thereunder, it shall be the duty of the Committee.—

(1) to arrange for—

(a) the upkeep and repair of the temple;

(b) the improvement of the temple land;

(c) the welfare and safety of the pilgrims; and

1 Subs. by para. 4 (1) of the A. L. O. for "Provincial".

(d) the proper performance of worship at the temple and pindadan (offering of pindas) on the temple land;

(2) to prevent the desecration of the temple or any part thereof or of any image therein;

(3) to make arrangements for the receipt and disposal of the offerings made in the Temple, and for the safe custody of the statements of accounts and other documents relating to the temple or the temple land and for the preservation of the property appertaining to the temple;

(4) to make arrangement for the custody, deposit and investment of funds in its hand; and

(5) to make provision for the payment of suitable emoluments to its salaried staff.

(Secs. 11-15)

Right of access and worship.

(11). (1) Notwithstanding anything contained in this Act or in the rules framed thereunder, Hindus and Buddhists of every sect shall have access to the temple and the temple land for the purpose of worship or pindadan. Provided that nothing in this Act shall entitle any person to perform animal sacrifice or to bring any alcoholic liquour within the temple or on the temple land, or to enter the temple with shoes on.

(2) If any person contravenes the provisions of the proviso to sub-Section (1), he shall be punishable with fine not exceeding fifty rupees.

Decision on dispute between Hindus and Buddhists.

12. Notwithstanding anything contained in any enactment for the time being in force, if there be any dispute between Hindus and Buddhists regarding the manner of using the temple or the temple land, the decision of the [1].[State] Government shall be final.

Committee to have no jurisdiction over proper

13. Notwithstanding anything contained in this Act or in the rules made thereunder, the Committee shall have no jurisdiction over the movable or im-

1 Subs. by para. 4 (1) of the A. L. O. for "Provincial" .

ties of Saivite Monastery. movable property of the Saivite Monastery of Bodh Gaya.

Audit of Accounts. 14. The[1] [State] Government shall every year appoint an auditor to audit the accounts of the funds of the Committee and fix his remuneration which shall be paid from the said funds. The auditor shall submit his report to the Committee and send a copy of if to the [1] [State] Government which may issue such directions thereon, as it may deem fit, and the Committee shall carry out such directions.

Constitution of an Advisory Board. 15. (1) The [State] Government may constitute an Advisory Board (hereinafter referred to in this Act as the ''Board'') which shall consist of such number of members as the [1] [State] Government may determine.

(2) The majority of the members of such Board shall be Buddhists who may not all be Indians.

(3) The members of the Board shall hold office for such term as may be fixed by the [State] Government.

(4) The Board shall function purely as an Advisory body to the Committee and shall discharge its functions in the . . . prescribed by the [1] [State] Government by rules made . . . behalf.

(Secs. 16-18)

Act to override Act 20 of 1863 etc. 16. This act shall have effect notwithstanding anything to the contrary contained in the Religious Endowments Act [1] 1863, or in any decree, custom or usage.

Power of the Committee to make bye-laws. 17. (1) With the previous sanction of the [State] Government the Committee may, from time to time, make bye-laws to carry out the purposes of this Act.

(2) In particular, and without prejudice to the generality of the foregoing powers, such byelaws may provide for:

(a) the division of duties among the Chairman, the members and Secretary of the Committee;

---

1 Priented in Central Acts, Vol Ed. 1951, p. 395.

(b) the manner in which their decision may be ascertained otherwise than at the meetings;

(c) the procedure and conduct of business at meetings of the Committee;

(d) the delegation of powers of the Committee to individual members;

(e) the book and accounts to be kept at the office of the Committee;

(f) the custody and investment of the funds of the Committee;

(g) the time and place of its meetings;

(h) the manner in which notice of its meeting shall be given;

(i) the preservation of order and the conduct of proceedings at meetings and the powers which the Chariman may exercise for the purpose of enforcing its decisions;

(j) the manner in which the proceeding of its meetings shall be recorded;

(k) the persons by whom receipts may be granted for moneys paid to the Committee; and

(l) the maintenance of cordial relations between the Buddhists and the Hindu pilgrims.

(3) All bye-laws, after they have been confirmed by the [1] [State] Government, shall be published in the Official Gazette, and shall thereafter have the force of law.

Power of Govt. to make rules.

18. The [2] [State] Government may make rules [3] to carry out the purposes of this Act.

[*Preface to the said Act*: "The Bodh Gaya Temple Act, 1949 (Bihar Act 17 of 1949) has been amended by the Adaptation of Law Order, 1950. The amendments made by the Adaptation of Laws Order have been incorporated in the text and some other foot-notes have been added for convenience of reference"— Deputy Secretary to Government, dated the 8th February, 1955]. [4]

---

1 Subs. by para. 4 (1) of the A. L. O. for "Provincial".

2 Subs. by para. 4 (1) of the A. L. O. for "Provincial".

3 For Rules under this S., See B. O. R. O., Vol. 1, Pt. VIII.

4 Government of Bihar, Law Department. The Bodh Gaya Temple Act, 1949 (Bihar Act 17 of 1949) [As modified up to 8th February, 1955],

Chapter XV

SOME IMPORTANT EVENTS (1953-1993)

Towards the end of 1952, the Bihar Government constituted the first Buddha Gaya Temple Management Committee consisting of four Buddhist and four Hindu members with District Magistrate of Gaya as ex-officio Chairman. The four Buddhist members in the first commitee were: Devapriya Valisinha, General Secretary of the Maha Bodhi Society of India, Ven. Bhikkhu Jinaratana of Assam, Ven. Bhikkhu Jagdish Kashyap, and Dr. Arabinda Barua. The management of the Maha Bodhi Temple was actually transferred to the new Management Commitee on 28 May 1953, the auspicious Buddha Jayanti day that year. According to a report published in the Maha Bodhi journal a gathering of over one lakh people, including Buddhist monks form India and abroad, witnessed the transfer of the management of the Maha Bodhi Temple by Mahant Harihar Giri, the Hindu Saivite Mahant, to the Joint Commitee of Buddhists and Hindus. The handing over ceremony held near the Temple was inaugurated by the Governor of Bihar, Sri R.R. Diwakar, and was presided over by Dr. Sri Krishna Sinha, Chief Minister of Bihar.

The Mahant's declaration of handing over the management of the Buddha Gaya Temple was read out by one of his disciplies. The 60-year-old Mahant himself handed over the declaration to the Chairman of the Management Committee, K.N. Sinha, Additional District Magistrate of Gaya. All the members of the Commitee, the Bihar Governor and the Chief Minister of Bihar, stood up in silence when the transfer was being made.

After the declaration, there was a recitation of Pali Sutta by Bhikkhu Saddhatissa followed by some extracts from the "Light of Asia" read out by J.C. Mathur, Secretary, Education Department, Government of Bihar.

In his Presidential remarks, the Chief Minister hoped that Buddhists from all over the world would come in large numbers to revive the dry fountain of Buddhist culture.

Dr. Sinha added that the link between India and the Buddhist world, which had broken some centuries ago, has been restored that day. He recalled the glory that Buddha had bestowed on the land of Bihar.

The Buddha Gaya Temple Act, 1949 had also provided for the constitution of an Advisory Board. It took the Bihar Government another three years to constitute the first Temple Advisory Board. Constituted in March 1956, the twelve-member Advisory Board included prominent Buddhists from India, Burma, Cambodia, China, Japan, Nepal, Sikkim and Sri Lanka.

The first meeting of the Advisory Board was held at the Maha Bodhi Rest House Hall, Buddhagaya, on the 17 March 1956, under the chairmanship of Sri R.R. Diwakar, Governor of Bihar. Dr. S. Radhakrishnan, Vice-President of India, inaugurated the Board. After the formal inauguration, the first meeting of the Board was held under the chairmanship of Sir Edwin Vijayaratna, High Commissioner for Ceylon (Sri Lanka). The composition of the Temple Advisory Board was later enlarged to include all the diplomats of the Buddhist countries also so as to make it a more representative Body. The Advisory Board provides a useful link between Buddha Gaya and the Buddhist countries who by now have established their own monasteries at Buddha Gaya.

The year 1956 marked a mile-stone in the chequered history of Buddhism in India. In that year, the Buddhist Era, which commenced on the day of the Maha-parinirvana of the Buddha, completed 2500 years. The Buddha Jayanti Celebrations of 1956 undoubtedly marked the beginning of a New Era, an era of hope and prosperity for Buddhism in India. To celebrate this historic event in a befitting manner, the Government of India appointed a Buddha Jayanti Celebrations Committee, headed by Dr. S. Radhakrishnan, Vice-President of India.

During the course of the year-long celebrations, thousands of religious and cultural functions were held and millions of pages were written in praise of the Buddha as almost all the Daily Newspapers and Periodical Journals in the country brought out special supplements devoted to the Buddha and Buddhism. In addition, hundreds of books and pamphlets were published in various languages of India. The All India Radio throughout the year broadcasted a number of features, talks and dramas on Buddhism. As was natural, on the occasion of the 2500th

Buddha Jayanti Celebrations, the Buddhist shrines in India got a face-lift. They were restored, repaired and renovated by the Government with a view to making the visit of the large number of Buddhist pilgrims from India and abroad more comfortable. Approach roads to these shrines were repaired; rest houses and canteens were constructed; and gardens were laid out. Thus the entire country during the year 1956 was swept by the Buddha-spirit.

The Buddha Gaya Temple too got a face-lift in 1956. The long needed repairs to the Maha Bodhi Temple and its precincts were carried out. Some more areas around the Temple were acquired; ugly hutments were removed and the surroundings were cleared up and dressed up. A preambulating path or pradakshina path round the Temple was also opened up. A small site Museum to house the ancient sculptures lying scattered near the Temple complex was constructed. In addition, amenities like electricity, water and accommodation for visitors were also provided. Yet another addition was the excavation and development of the Lotus Tank, to the south of the Great Temple. The Asokan Pillar, which was found at Gol Pather in Gaya, was also moved in 1956 to its present location in front of the Lotus Tank.

The greatest event of the year 1956 was the embracing of Buddhism by Dr. B.R. Ambedkar, alongwith half a million of his followers at a historic ceremony at Nagpur on 14 October 1956. A month after this historic event, Dr. Ambedkar visited Nepal to participate in the Fourth Conference of the World Fellowship of Buddhists held at Kathmandu from 15-21 November 1956. He received tremendous ovation at the Conference for his contribution to the revival of Buddhism in India. On return from Nepal, Dr. Babasaheb Ambedkar straight came to Buddha Gaya to pay his homage to the Great Buddha, his master, and worshipped in the sanctum sanctorum of the Maha Bodhi Temple, the Vajrasana and the Bodhi Tree on 23 November 1956. From Buddha Gaya, he came same evening by train to Sarnath where he stayed for three days before leaving by air for Kushinagar on 27 November 1956.

The transfer of the Maha Bodhi Temple from the Hindu Mahant to a Management Committee in 1953, followed by the 2500th Buddha Jayanti Celebrations in 1956 by the Government of India, and the mass conversion ceremony at Nagpur on 14 October 1956 created a stir in the Buddhist world, and the flow of pilgrims, including V.I.P.'s from abroad, suddenly increased. The first important visitors from abroad to Buddha Gaya were Their Highnesses the Crown Prince Akihito and Princess

Michiko of Japan. The 5th of December 1960 was a historic day as on that day for the first time in history the heir-apparent to the ancient throne of Japan visited the sacred site of the Buddha's enlightenment, and worshipped in person the Lord Buddha in the Maha Bodhi Temple, offered flowers, incense etc. and then went round the sacred monuments including the Vajrasana and the Bodhi Tree.

On this occasion, the Maha Bodhi Society of India also organised a public reception, which turned out to be the biggest welcome given to a foreign dignitary at Buddha Gaya and was attended by over 50,000 people. The reception was arranged in a pandal erected on the high ground to the west of the Temple. An attractive rostrum was erected on one side where the royal couple were seated, and formally wecomed by Palden Thondup Namgyal, the Maharaj Kumar of Sikkim and the President of the Maha Bodhi Society of India. Devapriya Valisinha, General Secretary of the Maha Bodhi Society, and Senior State Government officials were also present on this happy occasion.

Meditation plays a very significant role in Buddhism. One form of meditation is Samatha, calm or development of concentration. The other form is Vipassana, Insight, the meditation technique which was discovered by the Buddha at the time of His Enlightenment at Bodh Gaya. With the downfall of Buddhism in India, the Vipassana technique also vanished. Luckily, it was preserved in Burma, the country where the Theravada Buddhism still flourishes, and from there it was brought back to India in 1969 by Satya Narain Goenka, an Indian born in Burma, who had learnt the technique from his exalted teacher Sayagyi U Ba Khin, a great exponent of Vipassana meditation in modern Burma. Significantly enough, it was at Buddha Gaya that Goenka conducted continuously four ten-day Vipassana courses from 13 December 1970 to 26 January 1971. And it was at Buddha Gaya again that while conducting the fourth course, Goenka decided to establish a Vipassana Trust to spread the technique in India and abroad as was the wish of his Dhamma-guru U Ba Khin.

On 16 November 1974, a scene reminiscent of the days of Asoka the Great was witnessed at Buddha Gaya when U Nu, the former Prime Minister of Burma (Myanmar), his son, son-in-law and his Secretary were ordained as Samaneras (novices) under the Bodhi Tree. The ceremony, organised by the International Meditation Centre at Buddha Gaya, was proceeded by a colourful procession consisting of elephants, massed bands, flag and festoon bearers, saffron-robed monks and nuns of different nationalities and also a large number of Buddhist devotees from India and abroad, in which U Nu and his party were led from the Japanese Temple (Indosan Nipponji) to the Maha Bodhi Temple for ordination. And after circumambulation of the Great Temple thrice and offering worship (Puja) in the main shrine room, U Nu and party were led to the ground under the Bodhi Tree where they were ordained with due solemnity and admitted as samaneras into the Buddhist Holy Order, the Sangha. On the same evening, U Nu and others were given higher ordination, upasampada, at the consecrated hall within the precincts of the nearby Burmese Buddha Vihara.

His Holiness the XIV Dalai Lama of Tibet, who was forced to flee Tibet in March 1959, consequent upon the Chinese invasion, and has been living in India since then, often holds religious congretations at Buddha Gaya, the Holy Seat of Buddha's Enlightenment. Here we will confine our attention to just three of them, which were held near the Bodhi Tree in 1974, 1981 and 1985.

The Dalai Lama inaugurated the first Kala Chakra Initiation Ceremony at Buddha Gaya on 4 January 1974 in the presence of about one lakh Buddhist pilgrims assembled there. In his marathon discourse on the Dhamma, His Holiness asked those present to follow the teachings of the Buddha and cultivate the noble qualities of patience, humility, love and friendship. Verily, it was a unique gathering and the first such gathering at the holy site of Buddha's enlightenment.

Another mass religious gathering that His Holiness Dalai Lama XIV of Tibet addressed at Buddha Gaya was on 12-15 January 1981. This time His Holiness gave Commentary on the Thirty-Seven Bodhisattva Practices composed by Thogs-med brangpo, and The Three Principal Aspects of the Path by Je Tsong Khapa. In his opening remarks on the first day on 12 January, the Dalai Lama said:

> "Many people are here today from various places, even Tibet, and you have all come for the Dhamma purpose of listening to teachings. Therefore, concerning the development of Bodhichitta and so forth, I shall teach here in Bodh Gaya "Thirty-seven Bodhisattva Practices" by Thogmay sangpo and also "The Three Principal Paths" by Je Tzong-kha-pa. As we are in a very holy place, the merit collected here is much more powerful than elsewhere. But for this merit to be most effective we must have a very widespread and extensive motivation and attitude. This is necessary not only for the listeners to the teachings, but for the Lama or Guru as well.

The Enlightened Being, the Buddha, the Compassionate One, has a body with 32 major and 80 minor features and faculty of speech with 60 perfect characteristics. Furthermore, His mind is free from all delusions and obatacles such that He always has bare perception of Voidness and all phenomena exactly as they are. Such a Compassionate, Fully Perfected Buddha demonstrated His Enlightenment here in Bodh Gaya 2,500 years ago and we are all in this very place now." (Four Essential Buddhist Commentaries: 21).

The third time His Holiness the Dalai Lama visited Bodh Gaya was in December 1985 to perform for the second time the Kalachakra Initiation Ceremony. Over two lakhs of Buddhists from thirty-one countries including those from the Himalayan region of India and the Tibetan refugees in India and from abroad participated in the biggest religious ceremony performed by the Dalai Lama at Buddha Gaya. This was the biggest Kalachakra Initiation Ceremony ever performed by any Dalai Lama in the history of Tibetan Buddhism. Besides performing Kalachakra Puja, Dalai Lama also participated in a rare additional 'Monalm Chenmo' (greater prayer festival). Describing the scene on this occasion, an eye-witness account runs as follows:

"The maroon and saffron colours of the monks' robes set off the opaque whiteness at the foot of the Bodhi Tree whose broad foliage almost rivals the venerable stupa which stands on the place of the Buddha's Awakening. Rising from deep within them, and intensely alive, the prayers of thousands of monks weave a lattice of sound; they create a dimension of sacredness, and untouchable but invulnerable space on human ground. For hours the prayer pursued its lengthy ceremonial as the chanting rolled on between the tree and the temple, with one brief interval for tea, drunk the Tibetan way, with ghee and salt, and poured from big-pot-bellied tea pots held by a troop of smiling novices delighted by an excuse to stretch their legs. Another surprise in the midst of that magnificent Tibetan ritual was the interweaving of a Zen melody from Japan, a blessing from Korea, and an offering from Burma. At the foot of the Lotus throne the yellow robes of the Theravada bhikkhus (monks) stood out from the dark purple wave of the adepts of the Great Vehicle, the Mahayana."

"Finally the sun grew tired, and darted its last rays through the dust-filled air as if in tribute to the litany reaching upwards to the sky in the heat of an inner flame. One beat of a muted, incredibly sonorous gong threw a cloak silence. Thousands of faint candles were lit in the falling dusk, and suddenly it was night. Sculptures in butter gleamed in the half-night, and the grand master of ceremonies melted into the resulting tide of monastic robes for a moment, then slipped into the crowd, and, as he passed her, greeted Tara, protectress of Tibet since the dawn of Buddhist times, before leaving with a smile to return to the monastery.''

In the last 40 years, some significant improvements have been carried out by the Temple Management Committee. These include: (i) entrance from the eastern side, with proper gate and adequate parking place; (ii) a paved pradakshina path; (iii) inner and outer parikramas (promenades); (iv) replacement of the main door of the Temple by a teak wood door exquisitely designed; (v) a railing around the Bodhi Tree; (vi) gliding the Buddha image inside the main shrine afresh to suit the artistic taste with gold leaves; and (vii) the compound wall around the Temple with fixed iron grill around the Temple, with three massive gates, with iron shutters, on the east, west and north. All these improvements, additions and alterations have naturally enhanced the dignity and serenity of the Great Maha Bodhi Temple.

With a view to augmenting the funds required for carrying out repairs and renovation of the Great Maha Bodhi Temple and to improve its surroundings, the Temple Management Committee levied a renovation fee of 25 paise per head by way of entrance fee with effect from 28 February, 1977. The fee was payable by all the visitors, excepting Bhikkhus and Lamas, and children below five years. Later, with effect from October 1978, the entry fee was raised to fifty paise per visitor but the local devotees and local visitors coming between 5 a.m. to 7 p.m. were exempted. Some people resented the introduction of the entry ticket for the pilgrims to the holy temple, and in fact Ven. Dr. Rashtrapal Bhikkhu filed a petition against the Government of Bihar and the Management Committee in the High Court at Patna. Later on, however, this application was withdrawn by the Petitioner. The Order of the High Court of Judicature at Patna (C.W.J.C. No 25940 of 1978) reads as under:

Introduction of such ''Renovation Donation'' to the Hon'ble High Court of Judicature at Patna (ref. C.W.J.C. No. 2594 of 1978). The Order dated October 6, 1978 in this respect runs as follows: ''It is stated by learned Counsel for the State that the Collector of Gaya, who is the Ex-Officio Chairman of the Buddha Gaya Temple Management Committee in his Memo No. 2759/C dated the 29th September, 1978, has stated that the levy is not compulsory. Learned Counsel has produced a copy of that letter and the following lines from the same to support his contention — 'However, Buddhist monks, Hindus (Hindu Sadhus) and Sanyasis and other meditants (mendicants) have been exempted from paying fee. Then again, such visitors who refuse to pay this fee and are prepared to state that they are not in a position to make this token contribution, are allowed to enter without payment of the renovation fee. This position very well indicated that this is not a compulsory imposition and so the question of restricting entry of visitors to the Temple does not arise.'

From the aforesaid letters of the District Magistrate and Collector of Gaya, it is apparent that the levy in question is not compulsory and even those who do not pay are not prevented from entering the temples. In view of this position, Learned Counsel for the Petitioner prays for permission to withdraw this application.

This application is accordingly permitted to be withdrawn with the above observation." (Memo No. 6833 dated 8.11.78).

Whatever may be the arguments in defence of the 'entrance fee,' the levy of even a token entrance fee called 'Renovation Fund' can hardly be appreciated in the case of a living shrine like the Great Maha Bodhi Temple which is the most venerated Buddhist shrine, and where not only the devout pilgrims but even casual visitors donate generously inside the Temple. Moreover, the pilgrims, in particular, from the Buddhist countries contribute a lot from time to time towards the repairs and renovation of the Great Temple.

The most recent as well as the most valuable addition to the Buddha Gaya Temple is a golden railing and golden canopy around the sacred Bodhi Tree. Gifted by the Buddhists of Sri Lanka, it was opened on 16 January 1993 by the late President of Sri Lanka, H.E. Ranasinghe Premadasa. It was indeed a memorable and historical event that took place at Buddha Gaya in recent times. To mark the occasion, a vast area around the Maha Bodhi Temple — the roads, bye-lanes and the buildings were decked with Buddhists flags and brilliantly illuminated. The Maha Bodhi Temple too was adorned with festoons and illuminated.

In the morning of 16 January 1993, President Premadasa opened the first phase of the one hundred houses built for the poor at Buddha Gaya by the Government of Sri Lanka. In the afternoon, Premadasa opened the golden railing and the golden canopy by removing a curtain amidst chanting of Paritrana by Buddhist monks headed by Venerable M. Wipulasara Maha Thera, Ven. B. Pannarama and Ven. Dr. D. Rewatha Thero. After the recitation of the holy suttas, in Pali, the President Premadasa and Madam Premadasa offered their heartful respect and homage by touching the sacred Vajrasana with their foreheads. They were followed by others present on this occasion.

Later, the President of Sri Lanka addressed a vast gethering on the grounds opposite the Maha Bodhi Society of India building complex. Addressing the public meeting, President R. Premadasa said:

> "I had resolved to construct a golden railing around the Jaya Sri Maha Bodhi during my pilgrimage to Buddha Gaya in 1988. I also made a resolve to construct a golden canopy over the Vajrasana, the seat on which the Bodhisattva attained Buddhahood, on a visit to Buddha Gaya Vihara in October 1992. Fate has decreed that I represent my people to make these two offerings to Lord Buddha. There is no greater offering that we can make. All of us Sri Lanka Buddhists are overjoyed by this."

In the evening, the President of Sri Lanka and the party gathered around the sacred Bodhi Tree for 'Pahan Pooja' 'lighting of lamps' followed by a religious ceremony at the end of which Ven. M. Wipulasara Maha Thera delivered the 'Dhammanushashana.' He also thanked the President and the people of Sri Lanka for the noble gift — a golden railing around the sacred Bodhi Tree, and golden canopy over the Vajrasana, the Seat of Buddha's Enlightenment.

In fine, the Great Maha Bodhi Temple has during the last forty years (1953-1993) regained much of its lost glory, and is now a living shrine pulsating with life. Invariably, it is the scene of national and international Dhamma conferences.

The year 1994 at Buddha Gaya Temple began with a mass Prayer Meeting by nearly 5,000 monks and lamas, and as many lay men and women, drawn from all over the world. Organised by a U.S.-based Organisation of Tibetan Buddhism, these prayers began on a modest scale in 1989 but are becoming more and more popular. This year, the foreign participants in the prayers included Buddhists from the United States of America, Holland, Germany, Brazil, Thailand, Korea, Bhutan, Myanmar (Burma) etc. One lakh oil lamps and candles were continuously lit as part of the ritual throughout the ten-day World peace-prayers from 13-22 January, 1994.

May All Beings Be Happy.

Chapter XVI

THE MAHA BODHI TEMPLE TODAY

I Temple

Of all the Buddhist Temples built in ancient India, the Great Maha Bodhi Temple is the only Temple to survive through the ages. Of course, after the downfall of Buddhism in India, this Temple too had suffered a lot of damage due to the vagaries of nature and man, and was almost falling apart when it was repaired and restored thoroughly in the 1880's by J.D. Beglar, appointed by the Government of Bengal. As a result of that restoration work, and subsequent improvement, the Maha Bodhi Temple is now one of the most beautiful temples in the Buddhist world.

The Maha Bodhi Temple, as it now stands, is approximately 170 feet high, while its base is 50 feet square. It consists of a straight pyramidal tower surmounted by a stupa. Its entrance porch, comparatively later than the original Temple, is on the east. Each of the four sides of the tower presents several tiers of niches, while the front face has a tall lancet opening for the admission of light into the sanctum and at the base of the tower there rises a turret at each of the four corners — a miniature replica of the main spire. The Temple is built of bluish bricks, with a coating of plaster. In front of the main entrance, there is an imposing gateway decorated with delicate carvings. The Gateway presents on the front an elegant stone votive stupa of small proportions. The niches on both sides of the main entrance to the Temple contain images of the Buddha. The crowned Buddha in the niche on the left has two smaller Buddhas at its shoulders, while the Bodhisattvas Padmapani and Avalokitesvara stand at its sides. The Buddha in the niche on the right is particularly beautiful, and is dated from the seventh century AD. Both the Buddhas stand serenely on lotuses. In the portico there are two more Buddha statues on the left and right sides.

The central shrine room of the Temple, which is on the ground floor, is reached after passing through a vaulted passage. The pillars and the main door are made of stone. The great gilded image of the Buddha, in the earth-touching attitude (bhumi-sparsa mudra) symbolising the supreme event of Enlightenment, is enshrined in the main sanctum, the inner Vajrasana. It is the largest seated image of the Buddha found at Bodh Gaya. It is nearly 2 metres in height and shows the Buddha sitting on a patterned cushion instead of lotus; the earth goddess appears in the middle of the pedestal which is also ornamented with lions alternating with elephants. The beautiful statue of the Buddha dates from the tenth century AD. It was uprooted by the Hindu Mahant some time after the visit of Buchanan in 1811 but was brought back by Cunningham in 1880 and re-enshrined in its original place.

The upper storey of the Temple has two steep stone staircases on either side of the outer hall near the entrance. On the first floor one can walk right round the main tower as there is a wide and open promenade. At the four corners of this floor, there are four smaller towers which add much to the symmetry and grandeur of the whole structure. The two towers on the West side have small shrines containing images of the Bodhisattvas, while the other two shrines in the East contain the landings of the staircases. On the landing on the left side is a large standing crowned Buddha flanked by two smaller Buddhas, the one on the right subduing the elephant, Nalagiri. The landing on the right side also has a large standing Buddha. The statue has its hands in the gesture of bestowing blessings, and is flanked by Avalokitesvara on the left and Maitreya on the right. According to an inscription on its bottom right, it was donated by the senior monk of the great monastery of Somapura in Bengal (now Bangladesh). The inscription reads as: "The gift of the senior monk, Viryendra, well versed in the Vinaya and the resident of the great monastery of Somapura, an inhabitant of Samatata country and a follower of the excellent Mahayana school."

The parapet along the passage contains numerous stupas, some of which are exquisitely carved and those in the East are the best.

Under the main tower on the first floor is a fairly large shrine with a beautiful standing crowned and bejewelled Buddha dating about to tenth century AD. On either side of the main statues, there are two standing and two sitting smaller Buddhas, while two devotees bow at its feet. The figure of the Earth Goddess appears on the pedestal. The upper shrine room of the Maha Bodhi Temple has since been converted into a Meditation Hall for the convenience of Vipassana meditators.

The outer side of the Maha Bodhi Temple has innumerable niches, carvings, creepers, floral designs, birds holding a string of pearls in their beaks or makkaras having strings of pearls in their mouths, and images. The main niche on the west wall contains an unusually fine image of the Buddha.

The best view of the Great Temple may be had from the North.

II **The Bodhi Tree**

The sacred Bodhi Tree sitting under which the Buddha had attained Supreme Enlightenment, Sambodhi, is situated to the west of the Temple. Asoka's visit to the Bodhi Tree in the third century BC is known from his inscriptions, and is also portrayed in a sculpture on one of the Sanchi Gateways. The Bodhi Tree was cut down by Sasanka, a Hindu King, in about 600 AD, but luckily another tree arose from the same root. This tree was seen by the Chinese pilgrim, Hiuen Tsang in AD 637. However, in the course of a storm in 1876 the old Bodhi Tree fell down, and a sapling from it was planted by General Cunningham in its original place. This is the Bodhi Tree which we see today.

III **Vajrasana**

The Vajrasana or the Diamond Throne seen between the Bodhi Tree and the Temple marks the spot where the Buddha attained supreme enlightenment. The outer Vajrasana, a red sandstone slab, is 7 feet 6 inches long, 4 feet 4 inches broad and 3 feet high. Its top is decorated with unusal geometrical designs and there is a geese frieze around the edge. This is one of the oldest objects to be seen at Bodh Gaya, and was probably made by Asoka, the first Buddhist Emperor of India.

IV **Seven Sacred Sports**

After Enlightenment, the Buddha is said to have bathed in the Sakra tank. The two tanks which now exist, one in the Pipal Pati hamlet, south of Buddha Pokhara and the other in the Tikabigha hamlet, east of the former, seem to be the tanks of Sakra and Muchalinda respectively.

After taking bath in the Sakra tank, the Buddha sat cross-legged at the foot of the Bodhi Tree gazing at it for seven days, enjoying the bliss of Nirvana. He spent the second week in walking to and fro near the Bodhi Tree. The site of Buddha's Promenade (Ratana Cankamana) also known as "shrine of the Jewel walk," is along the northern side of the Temple. The footsteps of the Buddha are represented by lotus flowers on a narrow masonry platform about 53 feet long, 3 feet 6 inches broad and a little more than 3 feet high.

The Animisalocana Stupa within the court yard of the Temple marks the site where Lord Buddha stood, during the third week, gazing at the Bodhi Tree out of gratitude for giving Him shelter. The Ratanaghara or the Jewel-Chamber, a small roofless shrine in which Lord Buddha spent the fourth week in meditation is also within the courtyard to the north of the Cankamana.

The Buddha spent the fifth week under the Ajapala Nyagrodha tree where Sujata had offered him a meal of the rice-pudding. The actual site of this tree has not been identified yet, but a place within the premises of a Hindu temple in the village of Bakraur on the eastern bank of the Neranjara river is pointed out as the site where this tree stood. The site of Sujata Kutir is nearby.

The Buddha spent the sixth week near the Muchalinda lake where Muchalinda, the Naga King of the lake, is said to have sheltered the Buddha from rain. Mocharin, a village about a mile south of the Maha Bodhi Temple apparently derives its name from Muchalinda.

The Buddha spent the seventh week at the foot of the Rajyatana tree where He made His first converts, Tapussu and Bhallika, two merchants from Utkala, modern Orissa. From the Rajyatana tree, the site of which has not been identified yet, the Buddha returned to the Bodhi Tree and, after sometime, thoughtfully proceeded to the deer park at Sarnath (Isipatana) to impart the Bodhi to his former ascetic colleagues who had left him.

V Seven Other Objects

There are seven other objects of interest in and around the Maha Bodhi Temple Complex. These are: the Railing, a small shrine in the south-east corner of the Temple courtyard, the Votive Stupas, the Lotus Tank, the Asoka Pillar, the river Neranjara, and the site of Sujata's hut :

(i) A highly ornamented stone railing put up by lady Kurangi in about 100 BC was later re-arranged and enlarged to enclose the Great Temple by Raja Purnavarma, the last descendant of Asoka in Magadha, at the beginning of the seventh century. The additions made can be easily identified as the old stone railing was made of smooth sandstone, while the latter additions are of somewhat coarse granite. The Old Stone Railing had as many as 64 pillars. Of these, only seven pillars are now standing in situ, the rest having been either lost or removed to the Archaeological Museum, and replaced by cement casts of the originals.

The pillars of the Railing are decorated with a number of religious motifs, such as, a Bodhi Tree with umbrellas and garlands; a Bodhi Tree surrounded by a railing; devotees worshipping the Bodhi Tree; elephants worshipping the Bodhi Tree; a combined symbol of Triratana or "Three Gems" — the Buddha, the Dhamma and the Sangha — and the Dhamma Wheel set up on a throne and attended by two worshippers; the Dhamma Wheel alone; and a Deva flying over the battlements of city, with a garland in his outstretched hand, towards a Bodhi Tree before which a man is keeling in adoration.

(ii) In the southeast corner of the Temple is a small shrine with a large Buddha statue in bhumisparsa mudra, dated in late 10th century AD. This shrine is said to mark the spot where Brahma Sahampati appeared before the Buddha and implored Him to preach His Dhamma for the good and well-being of all.

(iii) There are a large number of votive stupas erected from time to time by the ancient Buddhist pilgrims. The best carved stupas may be seen inside the eastern side of the railing. Directly south of the Maha Bodhi Temple is the foundation of the biggest stupa ever built at Bodh Gaya. This stupa is said to have been built by Asoka the Great.

(iv) There is a large tank, known as the Lotus Tank, to the south of the Maha Bodhi Temple. In the middle of the tank is a statue of the Buddha sheltered by Muchalinda, the Naga King.

(v) A section of the Asoka Pillar may be seen at the entrance to the Lotus Tank. This uninscribed pillar was found at Gol Pather in Gaya and moved to its present location in 1956 on the occasion of the 2500th Buddha Jayanti Celebrations.

(vi) The river Neranjara, in which the Buddha had often bathed, and which He crossed on His way to the Bodhi Tree, is to the east of the Maha Bodhi Temple. The river Neranjara, now known as Nilajan or Lilajan, is now sandy and shallow for most of the time.

(vii) Prior to enlightenment, the Buddha was staying on the other side of the river Neranjara, in the area now covered by the village Bakraur. In that village are, therefore, the Ajapala tree, the scene of Sujata's offering, and the traditional site of Sujata's hut.

Another site associated with the Buddha, which still retains some of its ancient attributes of a sylvan retreat, is the Pragbodhi hill where, after the departure of his five companions and before moving on for meditation under the Bodhi Tree, the Buddha is said to have meditated in a cave, now known as Dungeshwari, for some time. The Pragbodhi hill is now known as Dhongra hill which, rising about a mile to the north-east of Bakraur runs on towards Rajgir.

VI Bas-reliefs and Carvings

The Old Stone Railing has also a number of interesting bas-reliefs and carvings, and they cover both religious and secular topics. The important subjects treated are:

(1) The birth of the Buddha at Lumbini.

(2) The Enlightenment of Buddha at Bodh Gaya.

(3) Buddha's First Sermon at Sarnath.

(4) Mahaparinirvana of the Buddha at Kushinara.

(5) The purchase of Jetavana by Anathapindika at Sravasti.

(6) Jatakas (stories of the past lives of the Buddha).

(7) Astronomical representations.

Here is a brief description of these carvings:

(1) The incident of Buddha's birth at Lumbini is depicted by the device of two mansions, one placed over the other. It is portrayed in the upper panel of the south-west corner-pillar of the Railing.

(2) There are four different representations of Buddha's Enlightenment at Bodh Gaya. The first three representations fill the upper panels of one of the corner-pillars of rail-posts and the fourth fills the upper panel of one of the corner-pillars. In the first representation, the Bodhi Tree alone figures with a quadrangular enclosure and without the Diamond Throne. However, it is honoured with two posted umbrellas and two hanging garlands. In the second representation, only the cubical seat is shown under an umbrella, with a pair of worshippers who are standing with joined hands. In the third repre-

sentation, only a quadrangular path of perambulation upon a colonnade pilasters is shown. And in the fourth representation, there is a two-storeyed temple with an open-pillared hall in the lower storey with a covered verandah in front. The verandah shows a sanctuary with the Diamond Throne enshrined in it. The throne is depicted as a cubical seat with a Triratana symbol placed upon it. The upper storey shows three small sanctuaries, each containing Diamond Throne.

(3) Of the six representations depicting Buddha's First Sermon at Sarnath, one fills a medallion in the middle row, three fill the upper panels of three rail-posts and two appear in the panels of two corner-pillars. The first representation is primarily an imitation of Asoka's Sarnath pillar, with the lion-capital with the wheel set vertically upon it. In the second representation, there is a chapel-like sanctuary with its arched entrance and lattice work and a cubical seat in front of pilaster bearing a wheel on its capital. In the third representation, there is a similar design excepting that the sanctuary has two arched wings on two sides with two hanging garlands. The fourth representation has a front-view of a two-storeyed building with an open-pillared hall in the lower storey and two chapel like sanctuaries with cubical seats in the upper. There is also a railing and wheel with a garland hanging from its rim. The fifth representation is also a two-storeyed building with an open-pillared hall in the lower storey with a verandah, and a cubical seat under an umbrella with a few worshippers in different attitudes of devotion. The sixth and the last representation of the First Sermon is a chapel-like sanctuary, in which a wheel is vertically set upon the lotus-capital of a pilaster.

(4) Of the eight representations of Buddha's Mahaparinirvana at Kushinara, six are in sandstone and two in granite. Some earlier designs present the stupa as dome-shaped and some as bell-shaped. Some have worshippers, as also flags, while others are without them. In one representation, the mound rests on a column with a lotus-pedestal.

(5) The purchase of Jetavana by Anathapindika of Sravasti at a fabulous cost by covering the entire park by golden coins, required for erecting a monastery for the Buddha is sculptured in the upper panel of a rail-post of the Railing. It shows one of

the servants carrying a basket full of coins to the two men who are spreading the square-pieces over the ground.

(6) The Jatakas (stories of the past lives of the Buddha) depicted at Buddha Gaya are — The Udanchani Jataka (No. 106), Silanisamsa Jataka (No. 190), Kasava Jataka (No. 221), Somadatta Jataka (No. 211), Asitabhu Jataka (No. 234), Sujata Jataka (No. 306), Sussondi Jataka (No. 360), Atthana Jataka (No. 425), Tittira Jataka (No. 438), Rohantamiga Jataka (No. 501), Kimchhanda Jataka (No. 511), Kumbha Jataka (No. 512), Sambula Jataka (No. 519), Alambusa Jataka (No. 523), Sonaka Jataka (529), Sudhabhojana Jataka (No. 535).

(7) The Astronomical representations are the Sun (Surya), Signs of the Solar Zodiac (Rasi-Chakra), and the Lunar Asterisms. The sculpture depicting the Sun or Surya shows a war-chariot drawn by four horses, two going to the left and the two to the right ; the driver with a turban as his headdress stands on the forepart of the chariot. Behind the charioteer and at some distance is a big disc like object under an umbrella. The representation of Surya at Buddha Gaya is the earliest representation in India.

The motifs of the Rasis or the Signs of the Zodiac are sculptured on the rail-bars and pillars of the Old Stone Railing. Of the twelve signs, only two have survived in situ. These are the Signs of Kanya and Tula. Here the Sign Kanya or Virgo has not been represented by the usual figure of a damsel in a floating boat holding a lamp in her hand, but by the bust of a garland-crowned and garland-wearing damsel. The Sign of Tula or Libra is represented by a typical Indian tradesman with a pillow before him. The other signs of the Zodiac found in the Buddha Gaya sculptures are those of the Sign Virsa or Tarus by a standing bull, the Sign Simha or Leo by that of a lion, the Sign Makara or Capricorns by that of an elephant-faced makara, the sign of Mithuna or Gemini by a pair of animals — a lion and a doe, and the Sign Dhanu by an Sagittarius by a bowman in the characteristic attitude of an archer in readiness to throw an arrow. The remaining Signs of Zodiac have since been lost.

Of the Lunar Asterism or Naksatras, only two have been found on the surviving portion of the Old Stone Railing. These are in the form of a horse and the other in the form of an antelope.

VII Archaeological Museum

The most interesting exhibit in the Museum is the stone railing that once surrounded the Maha Bodhi Temple. The major part of it can be seen in the courtyard of the Museum while a small section is inside. The carvings on the railing inside the museum are: (1) two figures worshipping the Bodhi Tree; (2). a Bodhi Tree surrounded by a railing; (3) three elephants worshipping the Bodhi Tree; (4) men in a boat picking lotuses; (5) the Hindu Goddess Gajalakshmi; (6) a temple enshrining the Dhamma Wheel; and (7) the purchase of the Jetavana by Anathapindika. On most of the crossbars are lotus medallions with human heads or with animals in their centres.

The Buddha Gaya Archaeological Museum has only a small collection as most of sculptures were either taken to other museums in the 19th century or were appropriated by the Mahant. Today there are as many as fourteen Buddha statues, besides other statues of Mahayana deities, in the custody of the Mahant. They are kept in the courtyard of the Siva temple in the Mahant's compound. There is also a large stone with the Buddha's footprints on it, and several stupas.

Summing Up

To-day, the Great Maha Bodhi Temple is once again a living shrine and is visited by millions of pilgrims and tourists every year from all over the world. And every year in May, the quiet town of Buddha Gaya echoes to the trump of thousands of Buddhists from all over the world on the Buddha Purnima Day marking the Birth, Enlightenment and Mahaparinirvana of the Blessed Buddha. On this occasion, the Temple and its precincts are beautifully decorated with Buddhist flags and festoons; and as the sun spreads its soothing rays on the 170 feet high Maha Bodhi Temple, a colourful procession led by monks in maroon and saffron robes from India and the Buddhist countries that have since established their own temples and monasteries at Buddha Gaya, and followed by a large number of lay devotees enters the Temple through the Northern gate and circumambulates it thrice after which the devotees sit under the sacred Bodhi Tree. Then they offer milk-rice and fruits and light candles near the 'Vajrasana,' the Diamond Throne, which is tastefully decorated with a silken carpet spread over it. Then follows the puja in the traditional manner after the administration of Five Precepts (Pancha-Sila) to those present there. After the puja is over, and prasad is distributed, hundreds of poor men, women and children are fed. The morning function comes to an end with a sermon by a venerable monk on the significance of the sacred day. In the evening, the sacred Bodhi Tree and the Temple premises are decorated with multi-coloured electric lamps which turn the Temple complex into a fairy land, and the holiest of the holy Temple shines the brightest in the moonlight of the Vaisakha Purnima, the Purnima that brings happiness to all.

An in the past so also now, the Great Temple is being enriched by the highest treasures, the most recent and the most valuable addition being a gold-plated railing around the Bodhi Tree and a golden canopy over the Vajrasana gifted by R. Premadasa, President of Sri Lanka in January 1993.

The prestige of the Maha Bodhi Mahavihara, the sole surviving symbol of ancient grandeur and glory of Buddhism, has been further enhanced by a number of modern temples and monasteries built at Buddha Gaya by the Buddhist countries.

Chapter XVII

BUDDHISTS SEEK AMENDMENT OF THE 1949 ACT

The Great Maha Bodhi Temple, the Holiest of the Holy Buddhist Shrine, is at present managed by a Committee constituted from time to time under the Bodh Gaya Temple Act, 1949 and the rules framed thereunder. In accordance with the 1949 Act, the Temple Management Committee consists of four Hindus and four Buddhists to be nominated by the Bihar Government, with District Magistrate of Gaya as its Chairman. However, in order to ensure that the Hindus have always an upper hand in the Committee, a specific provision has been made in the Act to the effect that its Chairman shall always be a Hindu. The relevant Section 3(3) of the 1949 Act says:

> "3(3) District Magistrate of Gaya shall be ex-officio Chairman of the Committee provided that the State Government shall nominate a Hindu as Chairman of the Committee for the period during which the District Magistrate of Gaya is non-Hindu."

As such, ever since 1953, when the management and control of the Buddha Gaya Temple was first entrusted to a Joint Management Committee, the Chairman of the Committee has been a Hindu. Not only that, even Secretary of the Committee, has always been a Hindu. Thus, the Buddhists have very little say in the management of their own shrine. The 1949 Act not only denies even bare majority to the Buddhists in the Committee but is an affront to their self-respect also as if per chance a Buddhist Officer is appointed as District Magistrate of Gaya, he cannot be allowed to function as Chairman of the Temple Management Committee.

And to add insult to injury, the Mahant is a permanent member of the Management Committee. He has even been allowed, illegally and unconstitutionally to retain control over certain structures, constructed by his ancestors within the Temple premises, in contravention of Section 3(I) of the 1949 Act which clearly empowers the Management Committee to manage and control the Temple, the Temple land and the properties appertaining thereto. As a result, even today the Maha Bodhi Temple is being desecrated by the Hindu Mahant at will. For instance, there is still an object of Hindu worship (Sivalinga) inside the sanctum sanctorum of the Maha Bodhi Temple itself, and the observance of Hindu rituals therein has become commonplace, much to the annoyance of the Buddhists. Just outside the main entrance to the Temple, there is a shabby structure known as the temple of the Panch Pandavas. Though the images therein are of the Buddha and His mother, Mahamaya, but the same are being depicted as of Pandava brothers and Draupadi by disguising them with clothes etc. And in one of the rooms of this so-called temple is another Sivalinga under worship by the Hindus.

Yet another form of sacrilege of the holy seat of Buddha's Enlightenment is the offering of pinda (Pinda-dana) within the premises of the Maha Bodhi Temple by the Hindus who go to Gaya to perform shraddhas of their ancestors. All this naturally spoils the serenity and aesthetic beauty of the Great Maha Bodhi Temple.

When, in 1891, the Buddhists first reclaimed their sacred shrine at Buddha Gaya, there were hardly 50,000 Buddhists in India, who primarily lived in the high Himalayan valleys and had practically no contact with the Mainland. By 1953, when the Buddhists gained partial control over the affairs of the Maha Bodhi Temple, India had still less than 2,00,000 (two lakhs) Buddhists. However, thanks to the lead given by Dr. B.R. Ambedkar, the modern Bodhisattva, who performed a miracle at Nagpur on 14 October 1956, India now has more than 50,00,000 (fifty lakhs) Buddhists. This has naturally instilled a new life in the Indian Buddhists.

The year 1991 marked the Twin Centenary Year; it being the year of birth of Dr. Babasaheb Ambedkar as well as the Maha Bodhi Society of India. Hence, the Centenary Celebrations of these two historic events in the history of modern Buddhism were celebrated with great enthusiasm by the Indian Buddhists and during the year-long celebrations, the one important question which came to everybody's mind was the liberation of the Maha Bodhi Temple from the Hindu dominance. It hurt their pride as it was a matter of shame that not only their most sacred shrine was controlled and managed by a Hindu dominated Committee but it was also still subjected to sacrilege and desecration by the Mahant and his henchmen. Hence, the question of realizing their unfulfilled dream of having complete control over the Maha Bodhi Temple assumed urgency.

The first salvo in this direction was fired by the local Buddhists of Buddha Gaya, under the leadership of Dr. P.C. Roy, at a Seminar on 8 and 9 December 1991 held at Buddha Gaya to mark the concluding ceremony of the Centenary Celebrations of the Maha Bodhi Society. It was, however, on 20 April, 1992 that the demand for complete control of the Great Maha Bodhi Temple took a concrete shape when the All India Bhikkhu Sangha at its session at Buddha Gaya passed a resolution demanding transfer of the management and control of the Maha Bodhi Mahavihara to an All Member Buddhist Committee. Soon thereafter, an All India Action Committee was formed at Nagpur, under the Presidentship of Bhadant Arya Nagarjun Surai Sassai, a Japanese monk settled in India, to liberate the Maha Bodhi Temple from the Hindu dominance. And on the Buddha Purnima day on 16 May 1992, a strong contingent from Maharashtra and other States converged on the Maha Bodhi Temple demanding total control of their holy shrine. The angry Buddhists even roughed up the priests of the Pancha Pandava temple in the premises of the Great Temple and damaged the earthen pitcher atop the Shivalingam in that temple. The protestors also hoisted the Buddhist flag atop the Management Committee office.

Simultaneously, the Government of Bihar was also requested by Ven. Dhammaviriyo Maha Thera, Member, Minorities Commission, and others, to make necessary amendments in Section 3 of the Bodh Gaya Temple Act, 1949 so as to provide for an all Member Buddhist Committee. The Chief Minister of Bihar, Shri Laloo Prasad Yadav, was kind enough to accede to this request, and even circulated a draft Bill envisaging an eleven Member Management Committee, consisting of ten Buddhists and one Government nominee.

In the meanwhile, the All India Mahabodhi Mahavihara Liberation Committee, Nagpur launched a Dhamma Yatra which began from the Chaitya Bhoomi, Bombay on 27 September 1992, under the leadership of Ven. Surai Sassai. Leaving Bombay and passing through Pune, Ahmednagar, Aurangabad, Buldana, Akola, Amravati, Nagpur, Baital, Bhopal, Sanchi, Gwalior, Agra and Palwal, the Dhamma Yatra reached Delhi, the capital of India, on 14 October 1992 where a grand rally was held. From Delhi, the Yatra marched forward and passing through Sankisa, Kanpur, Allahabad, Sarnath, Patna and Rajgir, it reached Buddha Gaya on 22 October 1992. A press report from Buddha Gaya published in the Times of India, New Delhi on 23 October 1992, reported as under :

1,000 Buddhists offer prayers at Gaya Temple

About 1,000 Buddhists were today allowed to enter the Mahabodhi Temple in batches and offer prayers. Led by the Japanese monk, Nagarjun Surai Sassai, the Buddhists, who had assembled here from all over the country, vowed to "liberate" the Mahabodhi Vihara.

Defying prohibitory orders, the demonstrators held a public meeting outside the office of the temple managing committee. Asked if he would seek international support, Surai Sassai said he did not need to seek it as it would be forthcoming on its own. He also told CNN in an interview that if necessary, the issue would be raised at the United Nations.

(Earlier, the Japanese monk had a meeting with the Bihar Chief Minister, Mr. Laloo Prasad Yadav, who assured that the issue would be resolved in 10 days, reports PTI).

Amid loud chanting, Surai Sassai, carrying the "Dhamma Jyoti," along with 32 other monks, vowed to "liberate" the Mahabodhi Mahavihara.

The leaders of the Mahabodhi Temple Liberation Movement also objected to the presence of the Shivalinga inside the sanctum sanctorum as it was not a Shiva temple.

The Mahabodhi temple was virtually converted into a police camp as CRPF jawans and policemen had taken up positions since early morning. Hundreds of special branch personnel in plain clothes were also deployed. The Shivalinga was cordoned off as the Buddhist marchers entered the temple after a hot exchange with the security personnel over checking with metal detectors.

The monks argued that passing through the metal detector was humiliating as well as against their religious beliefs.

Early in the morning, hundreds of demonstrators from Nagpur, Agra, Aligarh, Bareilly and Pilibhit walked to Bodh Gaya from the Gaya railway station. They were stopped 500 metres from the temple and were allowed to enter in batches of 10 and 15. The policemen did not allow the visitors to stay inside for more than two minutes.

Since, as promised by the Chief Minister of Bihar in October 1992 at the time of the Dhamma Yatra, no action was taken by the Bihar Government to amend the 1949 Act, the Buddhists again assembled in strength at Buddha Gaya at the time of the Buddha Jayanti on 6 May 1993, and held a rally demanding transfer of the Temple's management to the Buddhists. A press report from Bodh Gaya, dated May 5, and published on 6 May 1993 in the Times of India, New Delhi, reported the event as follows :

Buddhists hold rally in Bodh Gaya

> About 10,000 Buddhists led by Bhadant Nagarjun Surai Sassai, President of the All-India Mahabodhi Mahavihara Liberation Action Committee, marched through here shouting slogans as they expressed their "resolve" to "liberate" the Mahabodhi temple.
>
> The march begins a three-day agitation which will culminate with a dharna on Friday. Last October, Bhadant Sassai had led a Dhamma Jyoti Yatra from Bombay to Bodh Gaya demanding control over the temple.
>
> The district administration had to modify the prohibitory orders imposed yesterday as the marchers were willing to even violate the orders. The march began near the Burmese monastery and terminated at the Mahabodhi ground, passing the Thai, Bhutanese and Japanese monasteries. However, foreign monks did not join the procession.
>
> The marchers, many of them women holding babies, braved a temperature of 46 degrees Celsius and shouted full-throated slogans. Some marchers fainted and had to be given first aid. The protestors came from Nagpur, Pune and Akola in Maharashtra areas having a sizeable neo-Buddhist population. They also came from Agra and Pilibhit districts of U.P.
>
> Some complained that a large number of fellow protestors had been beaten up by the police at Itarsi and Jabalpur stations and taken off the trains.
>
> The Mahabodhi temple was baricaded and more than two dozen magistrates were deputed to maintain order. The District magistrate, Mrs. Rajbala and the Superintendent of Police, Mr. Sunil Kumar, personally supervised the security.
>
> An iron grill has been installed in the temple sanctum sealing the approach to the Buddha image and the disputed Shivalinga.

Bhadant Sassai said the grill infringed the religious rights of Buddhists.

Yet another press report on the events of May 6 at Buddha Gaya, published in the Times of India, New Delhi, ran as follows:

Buddhists irked by locking of temple

Lord Buddha's birth anniversary celebrations here today were marred by slogan-shouting as more than 300 monks joined Bhadant Nagarjun Surai Sassai in demanding Buddhist control over the Mahabodhi Temple.

Thousands of his other supporters from Maharashtra, Uttar Pradesh and Madhya Pradesh were stopped outside the temple's main entrance and allowed to enter in small groups after the monks came out of the temple. The police had a tough time controlling them.

The district administration had got the disputed Panch Pandava temple inside the Mahabodhi complex closed as last year some Buddhists had stormed the temple, beaten up the Hindu priest, disrobed the image and damaged the earthen pot covering the controversial Shivalinga.

The Buddhist protestors defied prohibitory orders to take out a procession today in support of their demand for a change in the Mahabodhi Temple Management Act, 1949 and transfer of the temple management to an all-Buddhist Committee.

At present a nine-member committee, with the Hindus in a majority, looks after the temple. It can be chaired only by a Hindu District Magistrate of Gaya. In the case of the District Magistrate being a non-Hindu the State Government is under statutory obligation to nominate a Hindu as the Committee's Chairman.

Bhadant Sassai had yesterday protested against the sealing of the Mahabodhi Temple's sanctum sanctorum a few days back and the district administration had unlocked it to allow the devotees to have darshan on Buddha Jayanti. However, the Shivalinga was cordoned off by the police to prevent its desecration.

This year the Buddha Jayanti celebrations were held on a low key because thousands of protestors descended here for a three-day agitational programme and all efforts were directed towards maintaining peace. For the first time the foreign monasteries did not take out a shobha yatra and the venue of the collective lunch for the monks was changed.

Though the year-long agitation by the Buddhists was not able to clinch the issue of transferring the management of the Maha Bodhi Temple to an All Member Buddhist Committee yet it succeeded in compelling the Bihar Government to take two major steps to ensure the sanctity of the shrine. The immersion of idols by the local population in the Lotus tank inside the Temple Complex, and marriages in the Temple's sanctum have since been banned.

But, the stalemate on the temple management issue continues even today (May 1994). The Chief Minister of Bihar, Shri Laloo Prasad Yadav, who initially showed sympathy for the Buddhist cause, appears to have developed cold feet, perhaps on account of political compulsions. But how long the Buddhists can be denied their inherent right to manage and control their holy shrine.

Since the Great Maha Bodhi Temple is the holiest of the holy Buddhist shrine, there is an imperative need to stop its sacrilege and preserve its sanctity. Hence, it would be befitting and appropriate if urgent steps are taken by the Government of Bihar to amend the 1949 Act so as to provide for an All Member Buddhist Committee for the management and control of the Mahavihara. As says Gurudev Rabindra Nath Tagore, "It is an intolerable wrong to allow the temple raised on the spot where Lord Buddha attained His enlightenment, to remain under the control of the rival sect." Hence, sooner the 1949 Act is amended, better it would be.

Chapter XVIII

NEW TEMPLES, NEW HORIZONS

For centuries from the time of Emperor Asoka there was a Buddhist colony at Buddha Gaya with a number of Viharas and Sangharamas where pious Buddhists spent their time in meditation and social service. Then, after the decline of Buddhism in India, such a colony ceased to exist and the holy shrine was deserted by the Buddhists in the thirteenth century. Later, the Great Temple was occupied by a Saivite Hindu Mahant who tumbled upon it by chance in the course of his travels in about 1590. And it was only in 1953 that the Mahant was ousted and the management of the Temple was entrusted to the Buddha Gaya Management Committee constituted under the 1949 Act by the Bihar Government. Since then, Buddha Gaya has developed fast and by now a number of Buddhist countries have established their own temples and monasteries at this holy place. As of now (May 1994), there are as many as twenty-one (21) Buddhist Temples and Organisations functioning at Buddha Gaya. These are:

1. The Maha Bodhi Society of India
2. Burmese Vihara
3. Tibetan Temple
4. Chinese Temple
5. Wat Thai (Thai Buddhist Temple)
6. Bhutanese Temple
7. Karmapa Tibetan Temple
8. Indosan Nipponji (Japanese Temple)
9. Daijokyo Buddhist Temple, and the Great Buddha Statue
10. International Meditation Centre
11. Tai Bodhi Kam Monastery
12. Vietnamese Monastery
13. Sakyapa Monastery, Mastipur

14. Buddha Vihara, Siddharth Nagar, Miyabigha
15. All India Bhikkhu Sangha
16. Nepali Tamang Buddhist Association
17. Root Institute

Under Construction

18. Buddha Foundation
19. Bangladesh Buddhist Monastery
20. Korean Temple
21. Taiwanese Temple.

Of these, only the first ten are being described here in brief:

1. The Maha Bodhi Society of India

When Anagarika Dharmapla first came to Buddha Gaya in 1891, the only Buddhist building there was a small rest house built in 1875 by King Mindon-Min of Burma for housing the Burmese delegation deputed by him to carry out repairs to the Maha Bodhi Temple. Naturally, therefore, the Burmese Rest House became the centre of his activities, and for the next ten years Dharmapala fought his unequal fight with the mighty Mahant from that small rest house. As the Mahant refused to give any land to the Maha Bodhi Society, it was only in 1900 that, a piece of land was allotted to the Society by the Gaya District Board on which now stands the Maha Bodhi Rest House. This historic building of modern times, which has served the cause of the Dhamma for over 90 years by now, was constructed by the District Board as a deposit work in 1901, and the cost (Rs. 15,000) thereof was contributed by the Buddhists of Burma and Sri Lanka in response to an appeal by Anagarika Dharmapala.

Ever since its construction in 1901, the Maha Bodhi Rest House has served as the office of the Maha Bodhi Society; provided accommodation to the Buddhist pilgrims from India and abroad and also served as a Watch-Tower to look after the safety and sanctity of the Great Temple. And since 1953, the Bhikkhus of the Maha Bodhi Society have also been responsible for performing the traditional Buddha puja and other religious ceremonies at the Maha Bodhi Temple. Since 1970, this sacred duty has been performed with great devotion and dedication by Venerable B. Pannarama, a soft-spoken and mild-mannered monk from Sri Lanka. The Maha Bodhi Society, under his able guidance, and in close cooperation with the Buddha Gaya Temple Management Committee and other Buddhist Organisations now functioning at Buddha Gaya, invariably organises the Buddha Jayanti and all other religious functions in the precincts of the Maha Bodhi Temple.

The historic Buddhist revival movement initiated by Anagarika Dharmapala in 1891 completed 100 years in 1991. The Centenary Year of the Society was celebrated with great enthusiasm and in a befitting manner by all the Centres of the Society. At Buddha Gaya, where the Society was born, a beautiful bust of the great Anagarika Dharmapala was installed in the premises of the Maha Bodhi Rest House on 23 September 1991. The bust of Dharmapala was designed and sculptured by Ven. Wipulasara Maha Thera, General Secretary of the Maha Bodhi Society of India, and all expenses thereon were donated by R. Premadasa, President of Sri Lanka.

Being ideally located just close to the Great Temple, and the Bus Stop, the Maha Bodhi Society at Buddha Gaya is the most convenient contact point for any visitor to Buddha Gaya. The Centre not only provides useful information and guidance to the tourists and pilgrims but also makes available books on Buddhism and Indology.

2. Burmese Buddha Vihara

The Burmese Vihara is on the old road to Gaya, just beyond the Mahant's Math, and near the Police Station. The shrine in the Vihara has a series of interesting paintings depicting important events from the life of the Buddha. The temple is built in the style of a small pagoda and is reminiscent of Pagan, the city of five thousand pagodas.

The old Burmese Rest House was the first building to be built by any Buddhist country at Buddha Gaya in modern times. It was built by King Mindon-Min of Burma (now Myanmar) in 1875 for the Burmese delegation deputed by the pious King to repair the decaying Maha Bodhi Temple. The old rest house was later demolished, and the present Vihara and the Rest House built.

The Burmese Vihara has a consecrated Seema where the monks can be ordained as per the Theravada tradition.

3. Tibetan Temple

The Tibetan Temple is to the east of the Maha Bodhi Rest House. Built in typical Tibetan style, its main shrine on first floor is stocked with many beautiful images, scriptures, thankas and religious objects. Its walls are painted in traditional Tibetan style with scenes from the life of the

Buddha and the Buddhist saints of the Mahayana and Vajrayana tradition. There is also a huge Prayer Wheel.

This Tibetan Temple belongs to the Gelugpa School of Tibetan Buddhism and was constructed by the famous Lama Khangauwang of Ladakh in 1933. This Temple has assumed greater importance in recent years as whenever His Holiness the Dalai Lama XIV (of Tibet), who has been living in India since April 1959, visits Buddha Gaya, he stays in this Temple.

4. Chinese Temple

A small Chinese Temple, built on the pattern of Buddhist temples in China, is situated further to the south-west of the Maha Bodhi Rest House. It was built in 1935 by S.T. Chhen, a Chinese Buddhist savant, and has some interesting paintings.

5. Thai Buddhist Temple

The 'Wat Thai' (Thai Buddhist Temple) is beyond the Chinese Temple, and to the west of the Archaeological Museum. It was first built in 1957, and later partially reconstructed in 1970-1972 by the Royal Government of Thailand. Built in typical Thai style and almost a copy of the Marble Temple in Bangkok, this temple is quite impressive and is an attractive building. The huge Golden Buddha in the main Shrine is its primary attraction for the visitors.

The Golden Buddha Image was installed at a solemn function on 3 May 1967. Donated by the Prime Minister Thanom Kittikachorn of Thailand, the Golden Buddha Image is 3.60 metres in height, and was flown from Bangkok to Gaya by a special U.S. military air-craft. From the Gaya aerodrome it was brought to Bodh Gaya in a procession by a large number of monks and laymen.

The procession was led by Venerable Phra Deb Visuddhimoli, Lord Abbot of the Thai Monastery. Before the image was taken to the Thai Temple it was taken three times round the sacred Maha Bodhi Temple, and the Lord Abbot made a special puja before the Vajrasana, near the Bodhi Tree.

From 1970 onward the Bhikkhu Sangha of India started holding yearly meeting at Wat Thai sponsored by the Thai Monastery.

6. Bhutanese Temple

Turning a corner and a little beyond is the newly painted Bhutanese Temple and Monastery. The foundation stone of this Temple was laid on

28 October 1983. The Bhutanese follow Mahayana Buddhism and belong to the Dukpa Kargyu sect of Tibetan Buddhism. Built by the Royal Government of Bhutan, this Temple presents a good picture of the rich spiritual and cultural heritage of Bhutan, the Land of the Thunder Dragon.

7. Karmapa Tibetan Temple

Across the road and down a little is the Kagyupa Vajrayana Buddhist Monastery, popularly known as Karmapa Tibetan Temple, of the Kagyupa sect of Tibetan Buddhism. The paintings inside it are in part copied from the paintings in the Mulagandhakuti Vihara at Sarnath.

8. Indosan Nipponji (Japanese Temple)

Beyond this Tibetan Temple and on the right side of the road is the beautiful Japanese Temple, known as INDOSAN NIPPONJI. It has been built by the International Buddhist Brotherhood Association (KOKUSAI BUKKYO KORYU KYOKAI), which was founded by various Buddhist sects in the whole of Japan in 1968. The registered office of the Association is at Nakameguro, Meguro-Ku, Tokyo. Its first President was Rev. Shoyu Iwaya, a renowned Buddhist priest in Japan. Under his dynamic leadership, this Japanese Temple at Buddha Gaya was planned and executed. As a first step of the project, the foundation stone of the International Buddhist House was laid in September 1968 and the work completed in February 1970. The construction of the Temple (Indosan Nipponji) began same year in December, and was completed in November 1973. The main door of the Temple was formally opened in the presence of a large distinguished gathering by Dr. V.V. Giri, the President of India, on 8 December 1973.

The Temple is a replica of ancient Japanese Wooden Temple and it gives a natural beauty without any artificial decoration and design. Interior of the temple wall depicts a painting based on some of the important events of the life of the Buddha. In the middle, an image of Sakyamuni Buddha has been installed which was brought from Japan.

A Japanese Pagoda was constructed in front of Wat Thai (Thai Buddhist Temple), Buddha Gaya by the International Buddhist Brotherhood Association in October 1965 on the land of Bihar Government. It has since been shifted within the premises of the Japanese Temple. The stone Pagoda, which is unique in India, has been designed and constructed on ancient Japanese tradition by expert Japanese engineers.

Bell of Dharma

In front of the temple, there is a bell tower hanging a big bell, weighing about 250 kg. The huge bell was presented by Mr. Kono Suke Motsewhito, Chairman, National Electrical Works Co. Ltd., Japan. Its schedule time of ringing from April to September is 5 a.m. and 6 p.m., and from October to March 6 a.m. and 5 p.m. respectively. Besides, the bell also rings at 12 noon throughout the whole year. The local people are also benefited in fixing their time for daily work due to the timely ringing of bell.

Bodaiju Gakuen (Bodhi Tree Kindergarten)

In the third step of its project, the construction of the kindergarten attached to the Japanese Temple was begun. On 8 December 1975, was held the ground breaking ceremony of Bodaiju (Bodhi Tree Kindergarten), a gift from the children and guardians of All Japan Buddhist Nursery and Kindergarten Association to Indian children. The Building was completed in February, 1977 although after giving the concerned training to the Vice-Principal of this kindergarten, it began running informally with 40 local backward and poor children since 15 September 1977 to 7 December 1977. In 1979, in the third year of its run the strength of children increased up to 50. The total strength of children in school is expected to be 120.

Children of three years and six months to four years get admitted through medical examination and psychological test. After completing two years course, they pass kindergarten for the primary education. As a result of this, almost all local, the backward and poor caste children for whom education is not normally within their reach, join primary school after passing kindergarten. The usual teaching time of kindergarten is 9.30 a.m. to 1.30 p.m. but during the summer and the winter it changes accordingly. During the four hours of stay children join TRISHARAN, PANCHASHIL in Nipponji, worship Nono Sama in kindergarten and, listen pre-lunch talks on various subjects, participate in programmes of language, music and rhythm, paper work/painting manual arts, activities in nature and so on in turn. They have facility of medical check-up, uniforms, educational materials, tiffin and other perks.

Komyo Free Medical Centre

The Japanese Temple also provides medical services to the visitors and local people at the Komyo Free Medical Centre which was inaugurated in December 1983, and has been functioning since then on a regular basis with staff and equipment complete.

International Buddhist Conference and Seminar

As per the cherished desire of the late Rev. S. Iwaya, the President of the IBBA and his associates, since 1975 the IBBA has been holding a seminar on different aspects of Buddhism on the occasion of International Buddhist Conference held at Bodh Gaya on 8-10 December every year.

The Organisation provides all the facilities to the participants of the seminar and conference. Every year the number of delegates is increasing enormously. The papers presented by the scholars are carefully edited and selected by the editorial board for final publication. Proceedings of every year is published before the commencement of the following session.

The International Buddhist Conference is invariably presided over by the President of the International Buddhist Brotherhood Association, Japan, and Dr. Arsta Tulku acts as Secretary of the I.B.C. This author was lucky to participate in two International Buddhist Conferences held under the patronage of the Japanese Temple at Buddha Gaya, viz. the 8th and 15th Conference held in December 1982 and December 1990 respectively.

9. Daijokyo Buddhist Temple

Just adjacent to the first Japanese Temple and on the other side of the road, another beautiful Buddhist Temple has been built by the Daijokyo Association of Japan. The Daijokyo Sect was founded by Rev. Tatsuko Sugiyama and its headquarters are in Nagoya, Japan. The term DAIJOKYO means the Great Vehicle of the Mahayana. This sect believes in the Lotus doctrine propagated by St. Nichiren (1222-1282) in the thirteenth century. The Daijokyo is lay sect and its rituals are simple and less elaborate and its priests are also from the lay people only.

The beautiful Daijokyo Buddhist Temple, with a lofty Pagoda atop, at Buddha Gaya was declared open by Giani Zail Singh, President of the Republic of India, on Sunday, the 13 February 1983, by cutting a ribbon assisted by Rev. Y. Sugisaki, President of the Daijokyo Sect of Japan. A large distinguished gathering, including Venerable monks from India and abroad were present to witness the opening ceremony. On this occasion, a special Puja was also performed in Japanese style in the shrine hall where the images of the Lord Buddha and Bodhisattvas are installed.

The First Anniversary of the Daijokyo Buddhist Temple was observed on 12 February 1984, and on the same day the Ground Breaking Ceremony of the Great Buddha Statue, the erection of which had been announced by Rev. Sugisaki in 1983 at the time of inauguration of the Temple, was also held. The Second Anniversary of the Temple was held on 23 February 1985 and was combined with offerings of prayers on completion of the foundation of the proposed Great Buddha Statue, and the inauguration of the Daijokyo Training School. The Third Anniversary was held on 19 January 1986 and combined with the Ground Breaking Ceremony of the proposed Daijokyo Rest House. The Sixth Anniversary of the Daijokyo Temple was combined with the completion of the Great Buddha Statue which was unveiled at a colourful ceremony by His Holiness the Dalai Lama XIV (of Tibet) on 13 November 1989 in the presence of a large distinguished gathering, including this author. Rev. Y. Sugisaki, President of the Daijokyo Sect of Japan welcomed the guests present on this historic occasion. Three-day unveiling ceremony, in which hundreds of Buddhist monks drawn from all disciplines performed Puja, concluded on 20 November 1989.

The Great Buddha Statue

Buddha Gaya, the sacred land of Enlightenment, now has the honour of having the tallest Buddha Statue in India. Erected by the Daijokyo Sect, Japan, the Great Buddha Statue is 80 feet in height and is 60 feet in width. It has been erected on a two acres of land acquired from the Government of Bihar, adjacent to the Daijokyo Buddhist Temple at the end of the road. Built of pink Chunar stone and seated on a lotus built yellow Chunar stone, the Great Buddha Statue is in the meditation pose with eyes half-closed. Erected on a solid concrete pedestal, the Statue is hollow type with a spiral stair case from the ground floor to the chest of the Statue—which makes four storeys. Wooden shelves have been provided in the interior walls in the three storeys of the Statue wherein 16,300 small Buddha images made of bronze sent from Japan have been enshrined. The construction of the Statue, which has been carved and erected by M/s Thakur & Sons of Chunar took more than five years from 1984 onwards.

The Tenth Anniversary of the Daijokyo Buddhist Temple was held on 9 November 1993 when the two statues of the two chief disciples of the Buddha—Sariputta and Moggallana—on the two sides of the Great Buddha, were also unveiled.

The Daijokyo Buddhist Temple, in addition to various religious activities, is also running a Sunday School in the Temple premises which is attended by 35 students from the locality. The children are taught to recite the Buddhist prayers, songs, drawing and Origami (Japanese art of making flowers, birds etc. with paper). They are also taught Hindi and English alphabets.

The Temple is also running the Daijokyo Training School since February 1985. This School is located in a separate two-storeyed building adjacent to the Temple. Here, classes on Typewriting and Tailoring are regularly held, and a large number of local students have undertaken training during the past years. The Typewriting Course is of six months duration and the Tailoring Course is for one year. Training is free and the students of the Tailoring class are even provided with necessary articles.

The Daijokyo Buddhist Temple, the Great Buddha Statue, the Rest House and all other activities being run by the Daijokyo Association are being managed efficiently by Shri M. Subba, who has been working as Manager-cum-Secretary of this unique institution since its inception.

10. International Meditation Centre

The International Mediation Centre, established by Ven. Dr. Rashtrapal, started functioning from 29 January 1970. It is the first full-fledged Meditation Centre at Buddha Gaya. Its old Centre is situated by the main road side on an area over five acres of land just opposite to the Magadh University. An imposing pillard Entrance Gate fashions its existence. The complex consists of a two-storeyed Meditation Building with seven annexies comprising of an office-cum-Library, a Pragyyananda Free Primary School, and Taugpulu Sayadaw Free Health Unit. From November 1993, an Orphanage-cum-Welfare Home has also been functioning at this Centre.

From April 1990, the International Meditation Centre has established another Complex which is very near to the Great Maha Bodhi Temple. The New Complex has an eight-roomed two storeyed guest house, a self-contained spacious Meditation Hall alongwith other annexures. Both the Centres of the I.M.C. have been adorned with meditative postured two beautiful Lord Buddha Images of enormous values gifted by the Most Venerable Bhadant Yanaviriyachan, Lord Abbot of Wat Dhammamongkol, Bangkok and Ven. Nun Kruapanich of Thailand respectively.

Born on 25 April 1930 in a pious Barua Buddhist family and ordained as a monk in 1953, Ven. Dr. Rashtrapal Maha Thera, M.A., Ph.D. Tripitaka Visharada is a reputed scholar well-versed in Pali and Buddhism. He is a prolific writer, and has about a dozen books on Buddhism to his credit besides more than a hundred articles and letters published in English, Hindi and Bengali periodicals and papers.

Ven. Dr. Rashtrapal Maha Thera is also closely associated with a number of other Buddhist Organisations. Since 1984, he is a Member of the Buddha Gaya Temple Management Committee constituted by the Government of Bihar in accordance with the Bodh Gaya Temple Act, 1949.

Summing Up

The erection of so many modern temples and monasteries by the World Buddhist Community at Buddha Gaya has not only enhanced the prestige of the Holy land of Buddha's Enlightenment but also transformed it into a Symbol of Buddhist Unity. The sweet sound of 'Buddham Saranam Gacchami, Dhammam Saranam Gacchami, Sangham Saranam Gacchami' reinforced by 'Om Mani Padme Hum' and 'Namo Myo Ho Rengo Kyo' recited daily in these temples certainly adds charm and spirituality to the congenial environment of modern Buddha Gaya. Verily, the New Temples have changed the face of Buddha Gaya and are indication of the bright future of Buddhism in India.

Appendix I

FUTURE DEVELOPMENT OF BUDDHA GAYA— SOME SUGGESTIONS

In spite of considerable improvement in the protection and preservation of the Great Maha Bodhi Temple during the last forty years, still much needs to be done. In particular, its sanctity is in peril as the sacrilege of the most sacred Buddhist shrine continues as heretofore. In my article entitled "The Great Maha Bodhi Temple — A Plea to Preserve Its Sanctity," the very first article in the Special Number of 'Sambodhi' published by the Buddha Gaya Centre of the Maha Bodhi Society in December 1991 on the occasion of the conclusion of the Maha Bodhi Society's Centenary Celebrations, I had suggested in the concluding paragraph as follows:

"Having regard to the sanctity of the Maha Bodhi Temple it will be befitting and appropriate if in the Centenary Year of the Maha Bodhi Society of India, steps are taken to stop the un-Buddhistic practices within the Temple Complex. Accordingly, it is suggested that:

(a) worship of the Sivalingam in the sanctum of the Maha Bodhi Temple should be stopped; and
(b) the building called Pancha Pandava temple should be dismantled and the Buddha images removed to a new building within the Temple Complex.

Further, all the Buddha images in the courtyard of the Siva temple in the Mahant's Math should be removed to the Archaeological Museum. It would also be reasonable and appropriate if the Buddha Gaya Temple Management Act, 1949 is suitably amended by the Government of Bihar so as to provide for an All Member Buddhist Committee.

The last article in the aforesaid Souvenir by K. Godage, Ambassador of Belgium also highlighted the need for proper restoration and preservation of the Maha Bodhi Temple. Since this article is much more wider in scope and the author has made therein some significant suggestions so as to preserve the sanctity of the shrine as well as development of its surroundings, the same is reproduced here in full for the benefit of all those interested in the development of Buddha Gaya:

RESTORATION OF BUDDHA GAYA

K. Godage

After a lapse of 23 years, I visited Bodh Gaya on pilgrimage. The intervening period has seen the erection of the giant Buddha Statue by the Japanese, the pavilions of Japan, Thailand, Bhutan and Tibet. Sri Lanka has a new Pilgrim's Rest and the Burmese Pilgrim's Rest has, like the country, deteriorated. Nothing else has changed.

The significance of Bodh Gaya to Buddhists and to India and Indians of whatever faith cannot be exaggerated, for Bodh Gaya is, without dispute, the place where India's greatest son achieved enlightenment. His thoughts and his message has influenced millions through a period of over two thousand five hundred years. The Buddha and his message form an eternal bond between Buddhists, the world over and India. It is for the above reasons that India becomes custodian and trustee for Buddhists world over, of the place most sacred to Buddhists.

Firstly, the Buddhist world owes deep debt of gratitude to that great archaeologist Lord Cunningham, but for whom this great place of worship would yet have been a piece of land, at the same level as the present road, to be built upon by shop keepers or dwellers. Sadly there is no recognition of our gratitude to Lord Cunningham, for Bodh Gaya has neither a monument nor a statue of him. It is particularly ironic that, this country, which erects statues for all manner of people, has not erected a monument to a man to whom India and the world, owe so much. Buddhist countries which have erected pavilions, statues at great cost have also failed to erect monument to this great man. They seem to have forgotten that the first act of the Buddha, after attaining enlightenment, was to stand before the Bodhi Tree to show his gratitude, even to a tree, for it had given him shade and protection at the time of his enlightenment.

Serenity: a word synonymous with the Buddha, captured in statues of the Buddha which adorn living rooms even of non-believers (only because of the serenity which the Buddha face exudes) is sadly lacking in Bodh Gaya. There is no appropriate ambience. The mood of the place is farthest from the serene. Immediately outside the Vihara premises is a bustling market place, where all manner of trade and services are being conducted. It is also teaming with beggars and touts, pickpockets and conmen.

It is ironic that, at a time when the Hindus of India are protesting the usurping of the birth-place of Lord Ram, the Hindus had put a 'lingam' inside the main shrine room at Gaya. Hindus (particularly the Brahmins, after having reconverted the Buddhists of the Asokan era to Hinduism) conveniently sought to incorporate the Buddha as the ninth avatar of God Vishnu and to deify him. Not only did the Buddha very categorically and lucidly denounce Gods, rituals and beliefs of Hinduism but he also attacked the very basis of its social system. Ironically almost vertically opposite the Maha Vihara is a sign post, indicating that the Buddha, in debate with a Hindu Sankaracarya had stated, (at that spot), that contrary to the Hindu belief that a man is born a Brahmin because of his karma and is also condemned to be an untouchable because of his karma, that by deed alone does one become a 'Brahmin' or an 'untouchable' and not by birth. He challenged the religious and social systems of Hinduism. Therefore, the Buddha's message was/is contrary to the Hinduism particularly of the Sankaracarya and the Brahmins. Therefore a fundamental difference between Hinduism and Buddhism and it is, therefore, not acceptable that the temple erected originally by the Buddhist emperor Asoka, to respect the memory and venerate the Buddha, should have at the centre of shrine room, a 'lingam !' This would have been considered a desecration but for the fact the 'lingam' is worshipped by the Hindus.

Another incongruous feature of Buddha Gaya are the hundreds of structures which have been erected in its precincts.

In the context of all that has been aforesaid may I therefore, make the following suggestions for the consideration of the authorities:

(a) Foremost architects, town planners of India, perhaps in consultation with counterparts in 'Buddhist countries' re-plan the town of Buddha Gaya with the objective of ensuring that it be restored to what it may have been like during and after the time of the Buddha. Keeping in mind the foremost fact that it is a place of worship and should, therefore, have an absolutely serene atmosphere.

(b) The shops, boutiques and dwellings that now surround the area should be removed to a point at least half a mile away from the main temple.

(c) The 'lingam' inside the temple should be removed and placed in another temple which should be erected near the river and a pipal tree, to respect the beliefs of those who consider the Buddha as the tenth avatar of Lord Vishnu.

(d) All structures, of no relevance to the Buddha's presence within the present precincts, should be removed and placed at a site outside the main Temple. The main premises would therefore only have the places of special significance in the Buddha story.

(e) The Government of India should declare an area of half a mile from the main temple, as a sacred area and no structures permanent or semi-permanent should be permitted within this area, other than perhaps a statue of Cunningham.

(f) The Government of India may consider setting up an international fund which would enable Buddhist countries in the neighbourhood and Buddhists the world over, to be associated in the restoration of Buddha Gaya.

Appendix II

THE MAHABODHI TEMPLES OUTSIDE INDIA

The Great Maha Bodhi Temple at Buddha Gaya was the most impressive and dynamic Buddhist Temple to be ever built in India. No wonder that in due course it became the most inspiring symbol of Buddhism, and the streams of pilgrims flowed towards it through the ages from India and abroad. It even inspired the Buddhists of Burma (Myanmar), Thailand and Nepal to build similar Mahabodhi Temples in their own lands.

The first and the most accurate replica of the Great Maha Bodhi Temple at Buddha Gaya was built at Pagan in Burma (Myanmar). Pagan is often hailed as the birth place of the Burmese culture. It was in Pagan that the first Burmese empire was founded. And it was in Pagan again that the renaissance of Theravada Buddhism began in Burma in the eleventh century under the dynamic leadership of Anawrahta or Anuruddha, the founder of the Pagan empire. When Anawrahta came to power in 1044 AD, the Upper Burma was following a very debased type of religion known as Tantric Ari. But in Lower Burma or Thaton, Theravada Buddhism was flourishing and in fact the king of Thaton, Munuha, had thirty copies of the Pali Tripitaka.

In 1056, Shin Arhan, a missionary Bhikkhu from Thaton came to Pagan and succeeded in converting the king of Pagan to Theravada Buddhism. Thereupon, it is said that Anawrahta asked the King of Thaton for a copy of the Pali Tripitaka but he refused. This enraged Anawrahta. He invaded Thaton; defeated Munuha, and annexed his Kingdom to his own empire. He also brought Buddhist books and monks to Pagan, and launched a vigorous campaign to spread the Dhamma. He established connections with other Buddhist countries; obtained relics, and initiated a great era of building pagodas dedicated to the Buddha. Anawartha's reign (1044-1077) is considered as the Golden Age of Burma as under him, the country not only witnessed political unification but religious purification as well.

As the royal patronage of Buddhism was continued by the successors of Anawrahta more and more Pagodas came to be built in Pagan. The most important Pagoda to be built in the thirteenth century was the Mahabodhi Pagoda. The Mahabodhi Temple at Pagan seems to have been built after a very careful study of the Buddha Gaya Temple, and it is very much similar to the Great Temple. In fact, according to experts, the Pagan Mahabodhi Temple is almost an exact replica of the Buddha Gaya Temple. Both the Temples are made of stucco. The general proportions of the Pagan Temple are close to those of the Buddha Gaya Temple, particularly the relative proportion of the towers in the podium. The ground-plans of the Pagan Mahabodhi Temple and the Buddha Gaya Temple are quite similar, and both the temples have cells in their central obelisks entered off the terrace.

The second Mahabodhi Temple in Burma was built in Pegu sometime in the fifteenth century. Unfortunately, the Pegu temple, locally known as Schewgugyi, is now mostly in ruins.

In Thailand (Siam), the first Mahabodhi temple was built in the major northern city, Chieng Mai during the reign of king Tilakaraja (1442-1487), who was a devout Buddhist and gave impetus to the spread of Buddhism in northern Thailand. Known as the Mahabodhi Arama or Wat Chet Yot, the Chiengmai Temple, had special relationship with the Sri Lankan Sangha. In 1455 AD a seedling grown from a seed from the southern branch of the Mahabodhi Tree at Anuradhapura in Sri Lanka was planted in the Chiengmai Mahabodhi Temple. The Chiengmai Temple is similar in design to the Buddha Gaya Temple but it differs greatly in dimensions. While the Great Maha Bodhi Temple is made of bricks covered with stucco, the Chiengmai Temple is made of laterite with a facing of brick and stucco, and its towers are very much reduced in size, especially the central obelisk. Another major change the Chiengmai Temple makes is by elongating the ground-floor cells into a rectangular hall and moving the main shrine to the cell of the central obelisk on the terrace.

The second Mahabodhi Temple in Thailand is in Chiengrai, a city some 150 kilometres from Chiengmai in northern Thailand. This temple was also built in the fifteenth century. It differs even much more with the plans of the Buddha Gaya Temple.

The fifth replica of the Great Maha Bodhi Temple to be built outside India is in the ancient city of Patan in Nepal. Known as ''Mahabuddha,' the Great Buddha, this Mahabodhi temple was built in the sixteenth century. According to a Nepalese chronicle, a Vajracharya, named Abhayaraj, of Patan went to Buddha Gaya where he stayed for a number of years. On his return, he constructed from memory a copy of the Great Maha Bodhi Temple in his home town. Begun by Abhayaraj in 1564, the Mahabuddha Temple is said to have been completed in 1601 by his grandson, Jivaraj. Each brick of the Mahabuddha Temple has an image of the Buddha.

SELECT BIBLIOGRAPHY

A. Primary Sources

1. Fa-hien	The Travels of Fa-hsien, Record of the Buddhist Kingdoms (AD 409) — Translated from the Chinese by H.A. Giles, Cambridge, 1923.
2. Hiuen Tsang	SI-YU-KI, Buddhist Records of the Western World (AD 637) — translated by Samuel Beal from the Chinese of Hiuen Tsiang, London, 1884.
3. Dharmasvamin	Biography of Dharmasvamin (AD 1234) — translated from Tibetan by George Roerich, Introduction by Dr. A.S. Altekar, Patna, 1959.
4. Rajendralal Mitra	Buddha Gaya, The Great Buddhist Temple, the Hermitage of Sakya Muni, Calcutta, 1878.
5. Alexander Cunningham	Mahabodhi or the Great Buddhist Temple under the Bodhi Tree at Buddha Gaya, London, 1892.
6. Benimadhab Barua	Gaya and Buddha Gaya, Volumes I-IV, Calcutta, 1934.

B. Secondary Sources

1. Ahir, D.C.	Buddhist Shrines in India, Delhi, 1986.
	Heritage of Buddhism in India, Delhi, 1989.
	The Pioneers of Buddhist Revival in India, Delhi, 1989.
	Buddhism in Modern India, Delhi, 1991.
	Himalayan Buddhism — Past and Present, Delhi, 1993.
	Gautama Buddha, Delhi, 1994.
2. Ambedkar, B.R.	Writings and Speeches, Vol. III, Government of Maharashtra, Bombay, 1982.
3. Banerjee, A.C.	Buddhism in India and Abroad, Calcutta, 1972.
4. Bapat, P.V. ed.	2500 Years of Buddhism, Delhi, 1956.
5. Barua, Dipak	Buddha Gaya Temple, Its History, Buddha Gaya 1975, 1981.
6. Bhattacharya, Tarapada	The Bodh Gaya Temple, Calcutta, 1966.

7. Coomaraswamy, Ananda K. — History of Indian and Indonesian Art, New York, 1965.

8. Dalai Lama, His Holiness the XIV of Tibet — Four Essential Buddhist Commentaries, Library of Tibetan Works and Archives, Dharamsala, Himachal Pradesh, 1982.

9. Devahuti, D. — Harsha — A Political Study, Delhi, 1983.

10. Dhammika, S. — Middle Land Middle Way, Buddhist Publication Society, Kandy, Sri Lanka, 1992.

11. Edwin Arnold — The Light of Asia, first published in 1879 — Reprint Theosophy Company (Mysore) Private Ltd., Bangalore, 1976.

12. Geiger, W. — Mahavamsa, English tr., PTS, London, 1934.

13. Hazra, Kanai Lal — History of Theravada Buddhism in South East Asia, Delhi, 1982.

14. Lal, R.B. — Bodh Gaya : Past and Present, Patna, 1953.

15. Lama Chimpa Alka Chatopadhyaya Edited by Debiprasad Chattopadhyaya — Tranatha's History of Buddhism in India — translated from the Tibetan, Simla, 1970.

16. Leoshko, Janice, ed. — Bodh Gaya, the Site of Enlightenment, Bombay, 1988.

17. Mitra, Mrs. Debala — Buddhist Monuments, Calcutta, 1971.

18. O' Malley, L.S.S. — Bengal District Gazetteer, Gaya, Calcutta, 1906.

19. Sangharakshita, Bhikshu — Anagarika Dharmapala — A Biographical Sketch, Buddhist Publication Society, Kandy, Sri Lanka, 1964.

20. Soni, R.L. — A Cultural Study of the Burmese Era, Mandalay, Burma, 1955.

21. Strong, John S. — The Legend of King Asoka, A Study and Translation of the Asokavadana, Princeton, New Jersey, U.S.A., 1983.

22. Valisinha, Devapriya — A Guide to Buddha Gaya, Calcutta, 1960.

23. Vidyarthi, L.P. — The Sacred Complex in Hindu Gaya, Delhi, 1961.

24. William Peiris — Edwin Arnold — Brief Account of His Life and Contribution to Buddhism, Buddhist Publication Society, Kandy, Sri Lanka, 1970.

C. The Maha Bodhi Journal

1. The Maha Bodhi — Maha Bodhi Society of India, Calcutta — Vol. I, May 1892 to Vol. 101, October 1993.

2. Maha Bodhi Society of India — Diamond Jubilee Souvenir 1891-1951. — Maha Bodhi Society of India, Calcutta, 1952.

3. The Maha Bodhi 1891-1991 Centenary Volume — Maha Bodhi Society of India, Calcutta, September, 1991.

4. Sambodhi— 100 Years Maha Bodhi Society of India — Maha Bodhi Society Buddha Gaya Centre, Buddha Gaya, December 1991.

5. The Maha Bodhi 1892-1992 Centenary Issue — Maha Bodhi Society of India, Calcutta, Vol. 100, January-May 1992.

6. Centenary Volume, The Maha Bodhi Journal 1892-1992 — Maha Bodhi Society of India, Calcutta, September 1992.

D. Others

1. Tulku, Arsta ed. — Buddhism and Human Values — Proceedings of the 15th International Buddhist Conference, 1990, Japanese Temple, Bodh Gaya, 1991.

2. Subba, M. ed. — Daijokyo Buddhist Temple — 10th Anniversary Souvenir, 1983-1993, Buddha Gaya, 1993.

INDEX

N

O

P

R

1. Map showing Buddhist Shrines in Bihar.

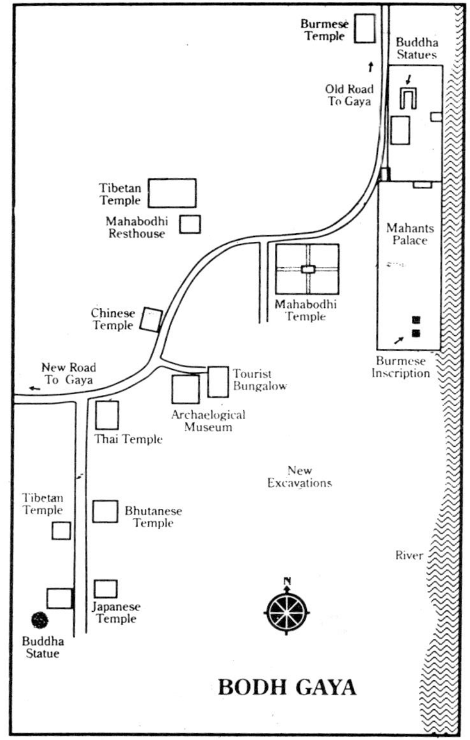

2. Guide Map of Buddha Gaya.

Courtesy : Ven S.Dhammika
Middle Land, Middle Way

1. The Great Maha Bodhi Temple

2. The Maha Bodhi Image

3. The Golden Buddha Image, Thai Temple

4. The Tibetan Temple

5. **Bhutanese Temple**

6. Daijokyo Buddhist Temple

7. Indosan Nipponji (Japanese Temple)

8. The Great Buddha Statue